simple stylish
KNITS

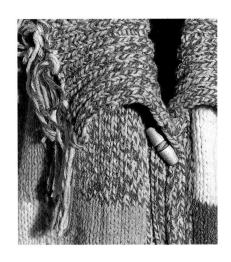

simple stylish
KNITS

A fabulous collection of
24 fashionable and fun designs

Hilary Mackin

NH
NEW
HOLLAND

First published in 2006 by
New Holland Publishers (UK) Ltd
London · Cape Town · Sydney · Auckland

Garfield House, 86–88 Edgware Road
London W2 2EA
United Kingdom
www.newhollandpublishers.com

80 McKenzie Street
Cape Town 8001
South Africa

Level 1, Unit 4, 14 Aquatic Drive
Frenchs Forest, NSW 2086
Australia

218 Lake Road
Northcote, Auckland
New Zealand

ISBN 1 84537 078 3

Senior Editor: Clare Sayer
Production: Hazel Kirkman
Design: Isobel Gillan
Photographer: Sian Irvine
Editorial Direction: Rosemary Wilkinson

10 9 8 7 6 5 4 3 2 1

Reproduction by Pica Digital PTE Ltd
Printed and bound by Times Offset, Malaysia

CONTENTS

INTRODUCTION

I have always had a keen interest in crafts. I can still remember our knitting lessons at primary school where boys and girls had to participate, and being the proud owner of my first knitted dish cloth made in a thick cotton yarn. I progressed onto scarves but don't think I actually wore any of my efforts. I can remember pestering my mother as to whether I was on a knit row or a purl row, which is exactly what my daughter does to me now. I was hooked. I grew up surrounded by people who made their own

clothes, knitted, embroidered, and turned their hands to soft furnishings. My granny, mother, sister and myself used to have thrilling nights sitting round the open fire, looking at knitting magazines and choosing what to knit or make next, and longing to go out to the local wool shop to choose the yarn, and the excitement of knitting that first row – even if it took a year to complete. Our hands were never idle. The knitting would appear whilst watching the television, or any spare moment during the day. Meanwhile my father would be working on another watercolour, away from the 'clickety clack' of the knitting needles.

Knitting is such a rewarding craft and has such tremendous scope. I have always been amazed at all the different textures and colour patterns that can be achieved from one pair of knitting needles and a ball of wool. As every stitch pattern is based on the simple knit one, purl one stitches, it never ceases to amaze me that by adding variations, such as cabling, you can produce such wonderful pieces of fabric. Two garments of the same shape can look so different by just altering the yarn, stitch pattern or colourway. Knitwear is comfortable and versatile, can look smart, casual or glamorous and is suitable for all seasons.

I hope I have communicated some of my enthusiasm for this wonderful craft. Whether you are using this book as a complete beginner or as a knowledgeable knitter, I'm sure there is plenty to inspire you.

Happy clicking!

BASIC INFORMATION

Equipment

Knitting requires very little equipment – all you really need is a pair of needles and some yarn and you are ready to go. However, there are many different types of yarn available now and a whole range of needles to choose from, as well as some other equipment that you will find useful.

NEEDLES

Knitting needles are available in aluminium, plastic and wood, although the larger sizes are only made in plastic and wood, as they are lighter and easier to hold.

Standard needle sizes range from 2 mm to 10 mm, although you will also find fat needles that are up to 25 mm (1 in). Generally, thick yarns are knitted using large needles and thinner yarns with small ones. The thicker the needle, the larger the stitch and the more quickly your work will progress. Needles also come in different lengths – choose ones which you find most comfortable to work with.

Cable needles are short needles which are pointed at both ends. They are used for moving stitches from one position to another when working cables.

Circular needles have two short needles which are each pointed and joined by a piece of flexible nylon which varies in length. They are much easier to handle than four double-pointed needles and are useful for neckbands or when picking up a large number of stitches around a front edge. They are ideal for any work which may be difficult to fit on a conventional needle.

OTHER KNITTING ESSENTIALS

Crochet hooks

These are very useful for picking up dropped stitches and working edgings on finished garments, as well as for casting off, joining seams and adding tassels.

Stitch holder

This keeps stitches that you are not using in place until you need them. You could also use a spare needle for this.

Tapestry needles

Blunt-ended needles with large eyes are used for sewing up items as sharp needles may split the yarn and weaken it.

Tape measure

Use a good tape measure – ideally one that doesn't stretch, as accurate measurements are important when checking tension.

Scissors

Have a sharp pair to hand for cutting lengths of yarn.

Row counter

This helps you keep track of stitches and rows completed.

Pins

Use long pins with large heads when pinning pieces together so that they will not get lost in the knitting.

KNITTING NEEDLE CONVERSION TABLE

Metric	British	American
2 mm	14	00
2¼ mm	13	1
2¾ mm	12	2
3 mm	11	2/3
3¼ mm	10	3
3¾ mm	9	5
4 mm	8	6
4½ mm	7	7
5 mm	6	8
5½ mm	5	8
6 mm	4	9
6½ mm	3	10
7 mm	2	10½
7½ mm	1	11
8 mm	0	12
9 mm	00	13
10 mm	000	15

Yarns

There is currently a huge selection of yarns available and choosing the right one can be daunting. You will find both natural and synthetic yarns as well as some synthetic mix yarns. Natural yarns such as wool and cotton are more expensive but they are often easier to work with. Synthetic yarns tend to be stronger.

Wool is easily available, long lasting and very warm. Merino sheep have the most abundant and highest quality yarn.

Cotton is strong, non-allergenic and easy to wash but is less elastic than wool.

Mohair yarn comes from Angora goats. The long silky fibres make it very warm.

Angora is like mohair, but softer. It is made from the hair of the Angora goat or rabbit.

Alpaca is less fluffy than mohair and angora; it is made from the hair of a llama-like animal.

Cashmere is the most expensive and luxurious of yarns, made from the fine downy hair of a special breed of goat.

Chenille is a velvety yarn made of tufts of cotton and synthetic yarn.

CHOOSING YARNS

All the patterns in this book specify which yarns have been used. To ensure the item appears the same as in the pattern, you should use the yarn that the pattern recommends. If you cannot find the same yarn, choose one of a similar weight and type and knit a sample to check the tension and appearance. When buying yarn check the ball band for the dye lot number and make sure you buy balls with the same number. See page 126 for more detailed information about the yarns used.

Getting started

GARTER STITCH

This is the simplest of all knitted stitches and is formed by working every row in the same stitch, either knit or purl, forming the same pebbly pattern on the front and the back making it reversible. It has a sideways stretch. If every row is purled, however, you do not produce such a firm fabric.

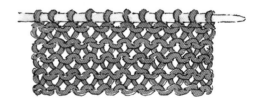

STOCKING STITCH

This is the smoothest of all knitted stitches, and is stretchy horizontally. It is formed by working alternate rows of knitted stitches and purled stitches. The smooth, knitted side is usually called the right side. When the pattern uses the purl side as the right side, it is referred to as reverse stocking stitch.

MOSS STITCH

This stitch forms a firmer fabric than stocking stitch and is created by alternately working knit and purl stitches. Stitches that are knitted on one row will be knitted on the next row and stitches that are purled on one row will be purled on the next row. For an odd number of stitches, the instructions will be as follows; K1, *p1, k1, rep from * to end. Repeat this row.

As this stitch does not curl at the edges, it is ideal for edges. It is also reversible.

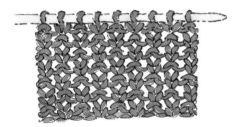

RIB STITCH

This is formed by alternating knit and purl stitches across the same row. The knitted chain stitch forms a rib and the fabric 'shrinks' inwards and has a strong sideways stretch. It is particularly suitable for cuffs and necks and body edges to form a neat, stretchable finish. It is usually worked on smaller needles than the main body of the garment.

TENSION

Making sure you have the correct tension is extremely important as it controls the shape and size of the knitted item. To make a tension swatch, knit a sample slightly larger than 10 cm (4 in) square using the same yarn, needles and stitch pattern stated in the pattern. Smooth out the sample on a flat surface, being careful not to stretch it. Using long pins, mark out the tension measurement given in the pattern, usually 10 cm (4 in). To determine the stitch tension of the knitting, count the number of stitches between the pins. Remember to include any half stitches over the width of a garment; a half stitch left uncalculated may amount to several centimetres in the final width.

To determine the length of the knitting, measure the number of rows. Place a rigid ruler or tape vertically along the fabric and count the number of rows to the centimetre. If the number of stitches given in the pattern knit up too wide it means the knitting is too loose and a size smaller needle should be used. If too small, then the knitting is too tight and a larger needle should be used.

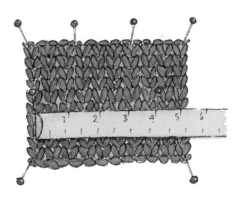

FOLLOWING A PATTERN

Knitting patterns are written in a language all of their own. Before starting to knit any pattern, always read it right through so you are familiar with the terms.

Abbreviations are used for many of the repetitive words that occur in the instructions. See page 10 for a full list of abbreviations; any additional abbreviations will be given with each individual pattern.

Asterisks are used to indicate repetition of a sequence of stitches. For example: *k3, p1, rep from * to end. This means knit 3 stitches and purl 1 stitch to the end of the row.

alt – alternate
beg – beginning
cont – continue
dec – decrease(e)(ing)
foll – following
g st – garter stitch
    (every row knit)
inc – increase(e)(ing)
k – knit
k1b – knit one in back of loop
k2tog – knit two stitches
    together
LH – left-hand
M1 – make one by picking up
    loop which lies between st
    just worked and next st and
    working into the back of it
p – purl
p1b – purl one in back of loop
p2tog – purl two stitches
    together
patt – pattern

psso – pass slipped st over
rem – remain(ing)
rep – repeat
RH – right-hand
RS – right side
sl 1 – slip one stitch
sl1-k1-psso – slip one, knit
    one, pass slipped stitch over
    the knit one
st(s) – stitch(es)
st st – stocking stitch, (knit
    row is RS, purl row is WS)
tbl – through back of loop(s)
tog – together
WS – wrong side
wyib – with yarn in back.
wyif – with yarn in front
yb – yarn back
yf – yarn forward
yo – yarn over needle
yrn – yarn round needle

Brackets are used where a set of instructions need to be worked a number of times. For example: [k3, p1] 4 times. This means that the stitches within the brackets are worked 4 times in total. Brackets are also used where instructions are given for multiple sizes; in the patterns figures are given for the smallest size first and the larger sizes follow in brackets. Where the figure '0' appears in a set of brackets, no stitches or rows are to be worked in that particular size.

The instruction 'alt' usually occurs during an instruction for shaping, for example: increase 1 stitch at the end of next and every alt row until there are 10 sts. This means that, counting the next row as row 1, the increase is worked on rows 1, 3, 5, 7 etc. until the required number of stitches is reached. If the instruction reads 'increase 1 stitch at end of every alt row' then the increases are worked on rows 2, 4, 6, 8 etc.

Care of yarns and garments

The correct after-care of all knitted garments is extremely important if they are to retain their original texture and shape. Many of the yarns available today are machine-washable and the ball band will clearly indicate where this is applicable. If in any doubt handwash in warm soapy water. Check the ball band to see whether the yarn can be dry cleaned.

When washing by hand, handle the knitting carefully and never lift the garment by the shoulders as the weight of the wet wool will drag the knitting out of shape. Squeeze out excess moisture gently without wringing. Support the overall weight with both hands and rinse thoroughly before drying to avoid matting. Spin dry for a short time only.

Never tumble dry a knitted garment. Knitting should be dried away from direct heat and laid out flat on a suitable surface. Spread the knitting out gently on a towel, and smooth out any creases. Leave until completely dry and then place over a line for final airing. Never hang knitting to drip dry. The weight of the wet fabric will pull the garment out of shape.

If a garment is properly dried it should not need pressing. If it does, check the instructions on the ball band. Some yarns may need steaming or pressing over a damp cloth. Never use a heavy hand when pressing knitted garments as this could distort the shape badly and never press ribbing.

Some yarns are prone to pilling during wear. This means that loose fibres gather into balls of fluff on the surface of the knitting. These can either be picked off, brushed or combed away, or go over the surface with a strip of sticky tape, sticky side down. Special implements can be bought for this purpose. If a snag occurs never cut it off; instead, take a blunt needle and push the snag through to the wrong side of the work. Gently tighten the yarn until the stitch is the right size and then knot the end on the wrong side.

Basic techniques

INCREASING AND DECREASING

Garments are most commonly shaped by increasing or decreasing the number of stitches in a row. There are many different ways of increasing and decreasing the number of stitches and each will create a slightly different appearance.

Increases and decreases are usually worked in pairs at each end of the row on the symmetrical pieces (back, sleeves etc) to give a balanced shape.

Yarn forward increase

To make the yarn forward increase in a knit row, bring the yarn to the front, take it over the right-hand needle and knit the stitch. The complete increase creates a visible hole and is often used in lace patterns. The increase is abbreviated in knitting patterns as yf (yarn forward).

In a purl row, take the yarn over the right-hand needle to the back of the work, then under the needle to the front. The abbreviation is yrn (yarn round needle).

Make 1 increase

Lift the yarn lying between the stitch just worked and the next stitch and place it on the left-hand needle, then knit (or purl) into the back of this loop. This increase is abbreviated as M1 (make 1).

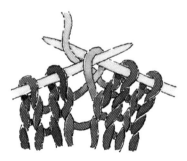

Slip stitch decrease

Slip the next stitch onto the right-hand needle without knitting it, then knit the next stitch. Lift the slipped stitch over the knitted stitch and drop it off the needle. This decrease is abbreviated as sl 1, k1, psso (on right side) and sl 1, p1, psso (on wrong side).

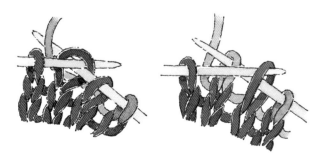

Working two stitches together

This decrease is worked simply by inserting the right-hand needle through two stitches instead of one and then knitting them together as one stitch. On a purl row, insert the needle purlwise through the two stitches and purl in the usual way. This decrease is abbreviated as k2tog (right side) or p2tog (wrong side).

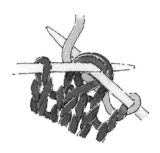

CHANGING COLOUR

To join in a new colour at the start of a row, insert the needle into the first stitch and using the new colour, make a loop over the right-hand needle. Pull through to complete the stitch and continue to the end of the row. Carry the yarn up the side of the work for narrow stripes but break it off and rejoin it for wider stripes.

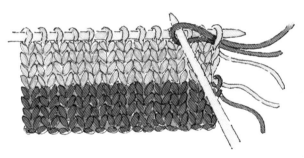

Where colours are worked in blocks, it is best to use a separate ball of yarn for each section. Twist the yarns over each other at the junction of each colour change to avoid a hole forming. When the colour change occurs in vertical lines, cross the yarns on both knit and purl rows. When the colour change is on a slanting line, the yarns need to be crossed on alternate rows.

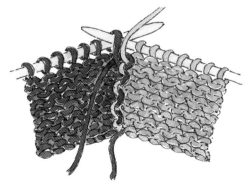

MAKING HORIZONTAL BUTTONHOLES

These may be worked on the main fabric or on a separate narrow band.

Work to the position of the buttonhole and cast off the number of stitches required for the width of the button and knit to the end of the row. Work to within one stitch of the cast-off stitches and knit twice into it. Then cast on one stitch less than was cast off and work to the end of the row.

Once the garment is complete, you can finish off the buttonhole by working round it in buttonhole stitch.

MAKING UP GARMENTS

Even the simplest garments require neat and careful making up so it is worth spending some time at the final stages for professional looking garments.

Before you begin joining pieces together, weave in any loose ends of yarn into a seam edge. Cover the pieces with a damp cloth and press gently with a steam iron – this will make them easier to join.

Joining seams

There are various different ways of sewing knitted pieces together but the garments in this book use the backstitch seam method. Use a blunt-ended needle.

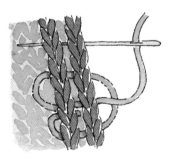

Place the pieces to be joined together with their right sides facing inwards, ensuring that the stitches and rows are aligned. Sewing into the centre of each stitch, bring the needle out one stitch in from the edge, insert the needle one stitch back and bring the needle out one stitch ahead of the emerging thread. Sew a few mm (¼ in) in from the edge of the knitting.

Joining sleeves

The top of the sleeve and the armhole into which it is set can often be different shapes so care needs to be taken when inserting the sleeves. Once the shoulder seams have been joined, fold the sleeve in half lengthways. Mark the centre of the top of the sleeve and the midway points between the centre and the underarm with pins.

On the main body of the garment, mark the centre of the shoulder join and midway points from that point and the underarm with pins. With right sides together, pin the sleeve into the armhole, matching up the marker pins. Using a backstitch seam, sew the sleeve seam on the inside.

Collars

Collars can either be knitted in by first picking up stitches around the neck edge or made separately and sewn on.

For a picked-up collar, join one shoulder as indicated on pattern. Divide the neck edge into sections and mark with pins to space the picked-up stitches evenly, then calculate how many stitches will be needed for each section. When working a non-reversible stitch such as stocking stitch remember to pick up the stitches from the correct side to ensure that the pattern is on the right side when the collar is turned over.

For a sewn-on collar, divide the neck edge and the inner collar edge into the same number of equal sections and mark them with a pin. With the right side of the collar facing the wrong side of the garment, pin the two edges together and sew.

Zips

Always insert an open-ended zip with the fastener closed to ensure that both sides match.

Pin the zip in position, taking care not to stretch the knitting. Use an ordinary sewing needle and matching thread. With the right side of the work facing, sew in the zip with a back-stitch seam keeping as close to the knitted edge as possible. Always work from top to bottom and take care not to cover the zip teeth. Slip stitch down the zip edges on the inside afterwards.

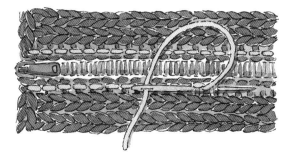

Decorative edges

These may be used to trim garments. They can be made separately and sewn on afterwards or knitted as part of the garment. Knit a length as indicated on the pattern, then with right side of edging to right side of garment, divide into equal sections and pin, sew in position using a back stitch. Allow extra ease for any curves on the main garment, so that the edging lies flat after sewing.

Making tassels

Cut out a piece of card the same length that you want the tassel to be. Wind yarn around the card to the required thickness. Thread a needle with yarn and pull it under the strands at the top of the card. Tie securely, leaving a long end. Using a sharp pair of scissors, cut through the yarn at the other end of the card. Wind the long end of yarn around the tassel several times about 1.5 cm (¾ in) from the top and secure by pushing the needle up through the middle of the tassel.

Fringing

Cut the yarn into the required lengths – just over twice the required finished length of the fringe. Fold in half and, with the wrong side of the fabric facing you, draw a loop through the edge stitch using a crochet hook. Then draw the loose ends of the strands through this loop and pull down tightly to form a knot. Repeat at regular intervals.

Sewn-on pockets

Use a slip stitch seam to apply the pocket, taking care to keep the line of the pocket and main fabric straight. A useful tip is to use a fine knitting needle, pointed at both ends, to pick up every alternate stitch along the line of the main fabric, then catch one stitch from the edge of the pocket and one stitch from the needle alternately. Make sure that the lower edge of the pocket lies in a straight line across a row of the main fabric.

ADAPTING PATTERNS

Sometimes it may be necessary to alter a pattern to suit your own body measurements. Working with the tension quoted on the pattern, calculate the amendments necessary to the stitches and rows and mark the alterations on the pattern.

CLASSIC

This chapter is full of timeless classics knitted in wonderful modern yarns, with features such as loop stitch, fringing and easy stitches. Wear with jeans for a casual look or be comfortably smart. There are ideas here for classic styling that would be ideal for any occasion – the office, out to lunch, shopping or days out. Win admiring glances when you wear any of the easy and quick to knit coats. The shawl-collared coat on page 26 looks fabulous when teamed with the striped sweater on page 32 – the colours complement each other perfectly.

This stylish coat is knitted in stocking stitch with garter stitch borders. It is surprisingly quick and easy to knit.

LONG ASYMMETRICAL COAT

EASY

 *Although this is a very easy garment to knit, the asymmetrical shaping requires accurate row counting.*

HELPFUL HINT

- To make sure the fronts are even, lay the garment out before sewing the front band in position. Sew with a back stitch, stretching the front bands slightly around the front edges above button fastenings.

MEASUREMENTS

To fit bust

81	86	91	97	102	107	cm
32	34	36	38	40	42	in

Actual width

115	120	125	130	135	140	cm
45¼	47¼	49½	51¼	53¼	55¼	in

Actual length

98	100	102	104	106	109	cm
30½	39½	40	41	41¼	43	in

Actual sleeve seam

43	46	46	46	46	47	cm
17	18	18	18	18	18½	in

In the instructions figures are given for the smallest size first; larger sizes follow in brackets. Where only one set of figures is given this applies to all sizes.

MATERIALS

- 12 (13:14:15:16:17) × 100 g balls of Rowan Big Wool in Tremble 035 (MC)
- 3 × 100 g balls of Rowan Yorkshire Tweed Chunky in Stout 554 (C)
- Pair each of 7 mm and 12 mm needles
- Buckle, 6 cm (2½ in) in diameter
- Button

TENSION

8 sts and 11 rows to 10 cm (4 in) measured over stocking stitch using MC and 12 mm needles.

ABBREVIATIONS

See page 10.

COAT

BACK

With 7 mm needles and C, cast on 65 (68:71:73:76:79) sts and knit 7 rows.
Dec row: (k1, k2tog) 6 (6:7:6:6:7) times, (k2, k2tog) 7 (7:7:9:9:9) times, (k1, k2tog) 6 (7:7:6:7:7) times, k1.
[46 (48:50:52:54:56) sts.]
Change to 12 mm needles and MC.
Cont in st st, beg with a knit row, work 104 (106:108:110:112:116) rows, ending with a WS row.
Work measures approximately 98 (100:102:104:106:109) cm (38½ (39½:40:41:41¾:43) in) from beg.

Shape shoulder

Cast off 5 (5:5:5:6:6) sts at beg of the next
2 rows, 5 (5:6:6:6:6) sts on the next 2 rows,
5 (6:6:6:6:7) sts on the next 2 rows. Cast off
rem 16 (16:16:18:18:18) sts.

LEFT FRONT

With 7 mm needles and C, cast on
33 (34:35:37:38:39) sts and knit 7 rows.
Dec row: K2 (3:3:3:3:4), (k2tog, k1)
9 (9:9:10:10:10) times, k2tog, k2 (2:3:2:3:3).
[23 (24:25:26:27:28) sts.]
Change to 12 mm needles and MC. Cont in
st st beg with a knit row. Work 5 (7:9:5:7:9)
rows, then inc 1 st at beg (front edge) on the
next and at this same edge on the 0 (0:0:3:3:3)
foll 8th rows [24 (25:26:30:31:32) sts], then
on the 9 (9:9:6:6:6) foll 6th rows, 33
(34:35:36:37:38) sts. Work 6 rows. Place a
marker at front edge on the last row. Dec 1 st
at front edge on the next and 12
(12:12:13:13:13) foll alt rows, then on the
5 foll 4th rows. [15 (16:17:17:18:19) sts.]
Work 3 (3:5:3:3:5) rows, ending with a
WS row.

Shape shoulder

Cast off 5 (5:5:5:6:6) sts at beg of the next
row, 5 (5:6:6:6:6) sts on the foll alt row. Work
1 row. Cast off rem 5 (6:6:6:6:7) sts.

RIGHT FRONT

Work as given for Left Front, reversing
shapings.

SLEEVES (MAKE 2)

With 7 mm needles and C, cast on 38
(38:41:41:44:44) sts and knit 7 rows.
Dec row: K2, (k1, k2tog) 11 (11:12:12:13:13)
times, k3. [27 (27:29:29:31:31) sts.]
Change to 12 mm needles and MC. Cont in
st st beg with a knit row, at the same time inc
1 st at both ends of the 13th (13th:9th:9th:
7th:7th) and 2 (2:3:3:4:4) foll 14th (14th:
10th:10th:8th:8th) rows.
[33 (33:37:37:41:41) sts.] Cont straight until
Sleeve measures 43 (43:46:46:46:47) cm
(17 (18:18:18:18:18½) in) from beg, ending
with a WS row.

Shape sleeve top

Cast off 6 (6:7:7:8:8) sts at beg of the next
4 rows. Cast off rem 9 sts.

POCKETS (MAKE 2)

With 7 mm needles and C, cast on 20 sts.
Knit 1 row.
Dec row: K1, (k1, k2tog) 6 times, k1. [14 sts.]
Change to 12 mm needles and MC. Cont in st
st beg with a knit row. Work 15 rows.
Inc row: WS. P1, (p2, M1) 6 times, p1. [20 sts.]
Change to 7 mm needles and C. Knit 8 rows.
Cast off.

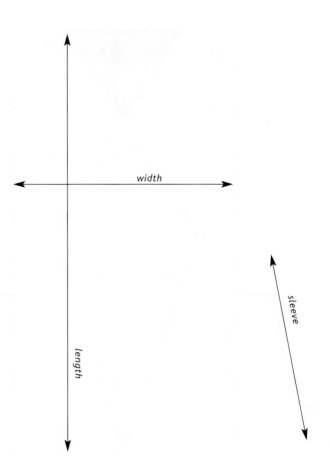

width

length

sleeve

POCKET SIDES (MAKE 2)

With right side facing, 7 mm needles and C, knit up 20 sts along one side edge of pocket. Knit 1 row. Cast off. Rep on other side.

TIES

Right front

With 7 mm needles and C, cast on 26 sts. Knit 7 rows. Cast off.

Left front

With 7 mm needles and C, cast on 10 sts. Knit 7 rows. Cast off.

TO MAKE UP

Join shoulders.

Front band

With 7 mm needles and C, cast on 7 sts.

Next row: Sl 1, k5, k1b.

Rep this row until band fits all round fronts and back neck edge. Cast off.

Sew on Front Band.

Attach Right Front Tie, positioning top corner to marker on Right Front, and under Front Band.

Position top of Left Front Tie, 10 (11:12:13:14:15) cm (4 (4½:4¾:5:5½:6) in) in from side seam in line with marker on Left Front, sew down top and bottom for 3 cm (1¼ in) and short end of Tie nearest side seam.

To cover the buckle, wrap the same yarn as used for the ties around the buckle and secure with a buttonhole stitch. Wrap other end of tie around inner stem of Buckle and secure. Sew a loop to edge of Front Band on Left Front so that the top of loop lies at marker. Sew a button to wrong side of Right Front to correspond with loop.

Sew pockets neatly to Fronts, positioning the bottom of the pocket 33 (35:36:38:40:42) cm (13 (13¾:14:15:15¾:16½) in) up from cast-on edge and 3 cm (1¼ in) in from side seam. Fold sleeves in half lengthways, place folds to shoulder seams and sew sleeves in position approximately 22 (22:24:24:25:25) cm (8¾ (8¾:9½:9½:9¾:9¾) in) from top of shoulder. Join side and sleeve seams. Pin out garment to the measurement given on page 16. Cover with damp cloths and leave until dry.

Although this is a large garment it can be knitted up very quickly. The attractive basketweave fabric is really easy to create and the large sailor collar and tassels are the perfect details. To top it all you can knit a matching beret.

BASKETWEAVE COAT AND HAT

★★☆ EASY

 Some experience is needed to create the basketweave fabric.

This garment requires neat making up.

MEASUREMENTS

To fit bust

| 81–86 | 91–97 | 102–107 | 112–117 | 122–127 | cm |
| 32–34 | 36–38 | 40–42 | 44–46 | 48–50 | in |

Actual width

| 110 | 123 | 130 | 143 | 150 | cm |
| 43½ | 48½ | 51¼ | 56¼ | 59 | in |

Actual length

| 102 | 107 | 112 | 117 | 122 | cm |
| 40 | 42 | 44 | 46 | 48 | in |

Actual sleeve seam

| 42 | 42 | 42 | 44 | 44 | cm |
| 16½ | 16½ | 16½ | 17½ | 17½ | in |

In the instructions figures are given for the smallest size first; larger sizes follow in brackets. Where only one set of figures is given this applies to all sizes.

MATERIALS

For the coat
- 18 (19:20:21:22) × 100 g balls of Sirdar Bigga in Blue Suede 694
- Pair of 15 mm needles
- Stitch holders
- 3 buttons

For the hat
- 2 × 100 g balls of Sirdar Bigga in Blue Suede 694
- Pair of 15 mm needles

TENSION

6 sts and 9 rows to 10 cm (4 in) measured over stocking stitch using 15 mm needles.

ABBREVIATIONS

See page 10.

COAT

BACK

With 15 mm needles cast on 33 (37:39:43:45) sts.
Row 1: RS. *K1, p1; rep from * to last st, k1.
Row 2: *P1, k1; rep from * to last st, p1.
These 2 rows form the rib. Work 4 more rows in rib.
Cont in main patt as follows:
Row 1: RS. Knit.
Row 2: K3 (5:2:4:5), *p3, k5; rep from * to last 6 (8:5:7:8) sts, p3, k3 (5:2:4:5).
Row 3: P3 (5:2:4:5), *k3, p5; rep from * to last 6 (8:5:7:8) sts, k3, p3 (5:2:4:5).
Row 4: As Row 2.
Row 5: Knit.
Row 6: P2 (0:1:3:0), k5 (1:5:5:1), *p3, k5; rep from * to last 10 (4:9:11:4) sts, p3, k5 (1:5:5:1), p2 (0:1:3:0).
Row 7: K2 (0:1:3:0), p5 (1:5:5:1), *k3, p5; rep from * to last 10 (4:9:11:4) sts, k3, p5 (1:5:5:1), k2 (0:1:3:0).
Row 8: As Row 6.
These 8 rows form the main patt and are repeated throughout.

HELPFUL HINT

When buying yarn, check the ball band for the dye lot number. Different dye lot numbers means that the colours may differ slightly so make sure you buy the correct number of balls with the same dye lot number – especially when you are knitting up a large project such as this one.

Cont in patt until work measures 102 (107:112:117:122) cm (40 (42:44:46:48) in) from beg, ending with a WS row.

Shape shoulders

Cast off 6 (7:7:8:8) sts at beg of the next 2 rows. [21 (23:25:27:29) sts.]
Cast off 6 (7:8:8:9) sts at beg of the next 2 rows. Cast off rem 9 (9:9:11:11) sts.

POCKET LININGS (MAKE 2)

With 15 mm needles and using the thumb method, cast on 11 sts. Work 16 rows in st st beg with a knit row. Leave sts on a st holder.

LEFT FRONT

With 15 mm needles cast on 20 (22:24:26:28) sts and work 6 rows in rib as follows:
Row 1: RS. *K1, p1; rep from * to last 2 sts, k1, k1b.
Row 2: Sl 1, *p1, k1; rep from * to last st, p1. Work 4 more rows in rib.
Cont in main patt as follows:
Row 1: RS. Knit to the last 4 sts, k1, p1, k1, k1b (these last 4 sts form the front band).
Row 2: Sl 1, p1, k1, p1 (these 4 sts form the front band), p0 (0:2:2:3), k2 (2:5:5:5), p3, k5, p3, k3 (5:2:4:5).
Row 3: P3 (5:2:4:5), k3, p5, k3, p2 (2:5:5:5), k0 (0:2:2:3), k1, p1, k1, k1b.
Row 4: As Row 2.

Row 5: Knit to the last 4 sts, k1, p1, k1, k1b.
Row 6: Sl 1, p1, k1, p1, k0 (0:3:3:4), p1 (1:3:3:3), k5, p3, k5, p2 (3:1:3:3), k0 (1:0:0:1).
Row 7: P0 (3:0:0:1), k2 (3:1:3:3), p5, k3, p5, k1 (1:3:3:3), p0 (0:3:3:4), k1, p1, k1, k1b.
Row 8: As Row 6.
Cont straight in patt as now set until work measures 53 (58:62:66:70) cm (21 (23:24½:26:27½) in) from beg, ending with a WS row.

Place pocket

Patt 3 (4:5:6:7), slip the next 11 sts on a st holder and patt across 11 sts from one st holder for pocket lining, patt 2 (3:4:5:6), k1, p1, k1, k1b.
Cont straight in patt on these sts until Front measures 22 (24:26:28:30) rows shorter than Back to beg of shoulder shaping, ending with a WS row. **

Work rib for collar

Row 1: Patt to last 7 sts, work 2tog, k1, M1, rib to end.
Row 2: Sl 1, rib 4, M1, p1, patt to end.
Row 3: Patt to last 9 sts, work 2tog, k1, M1, rib to end.
Row 4: Sl 1, rib 6, M1, p1, patt to end.
Row 5: Patt to last 11 sts, work 2tog, k1, M1, rib to end.
Row 6: Sl 1, rib 8, M1, p1, patt to end.

Row 7: Patt to last 13 sts, work 2tog, k1, M1, rib to end.

Row 8: Sl 1, rib 10, M1, p1, patt to end.

Row 9: Patt to last 15 sts, work 2tog, k1, M1, rib to end.

Row 10: Sl 1, rib 12, M1, p1, patt to end. [25 (27:29:31:33) sts.]

2nd, 3rd, 4th and 5th sizes

Row 11: Patt to last 17 sts, work 2tog, k1, M1, rib to end.

Row 12: Sl 1, rib 14, M1, p1, patt to end. [(28:30:32:34) sts.]

3rd, 4th and 5th sizes

Row 13: Patt to last 19 sts, work 2tog, k1, M1, rib to end.

Row 14: Sl 1, rib 16, M1, p1, patt to end. [(31:33:35) sts.]

4th and 5th sizes

Row 15: Patt to last 21 sts, work 2tog, k1, M1, rib to end.

Row 16: Sl 1, rib 18, M1, p1, patt to end. [(34:36) sts.]

5th size

Row 17: Patt to last 23 sts, work2tog, k1, M1, rib to end.

Row 18: Sl 1, rib 20, M1, p1, patt to end. [37 sts.]

All sizes

Cont straight in patt as now set until work measures same as Back to beg of shoulder shaping, ending with a WS row.

Shape shoulder

Cast off 6 (7:7:8:8) sts at beg of the next row [19 (21:24:26:29) sts], 6 (7:8:8:9) sts on the foll alt row ending with a RS row. Leave rem 13 (14:16:18:20) sts on a st holder.

Place markers for 3 buttons on front band, the first to come 41 (44:48:52:56) cm (16 (17½:19:20½:22) in) up from cast-on edge, the last 3 cm (1¼ in) down from beg of rib for collar and the remaining spaced evenly between.

RIGHT FRONT

With 15 mm needles cast on 20 (22:24:26:28) sts and work 6 rows in rib as follows:

Row 1: RS. Sl 1, *k1, p1; rep from * to last st, k1.

Row 2: *P1, k1; rep from * to last 2 sts, p1, k1b.

Cont in main patt placing patt as follows:

Row 1: Sl 1, k1, p1, k1, knit to end.

Row 2: K3 (5:2:4:5), p3, k5, p3, k2 (2:5:5:5), p0 (0:2:2:3), p1, k1, p1, k1b.

Row 3: Sl 1, k1, p1, k1, k0 (0:2:2:3), p2 (2:5:5:5), k3, p5, k3, p3 (5:2:4:5).

Row 4: As Row 2.

Row 5: Sl 1, k1, p1, k1, knit to end.

Row 6: K0 (1:0:0:1), p2 (3:1:3:3), k5, p3, k5, p1 (1:3:3:3), k0 (0:3:3:4), p1, k1, p1, k1b.

Row 7: Sl 1, k1, p1, k1, p0 (0:3:3:4), k1 (1:3:3:3), p5, k3, p5, k2 (3:1:3:3), p0 (1:0:0:1).

Row 8: As Row 6.

Cont straight in patt as now set making buttonholes in front band to correspond with markers on Left Front as follows:

Buttonhole row – right side
Sl 1, k1, yo, k2tog, patt to end.
Place pocket when work measures 53 (58:62:66:70) cm (21 (23:24½:26:27½) in) from beg, ending with a WS row.

Place pocket
Next row: Sl 1, k1, p1, k1, patt 2 (3:4:5:6), sl the next 11 sts on a st holder and patt across 11 sts from rem pocket st holder, patt rem 3 (4:5:6:7) sts.
Cont straight in patt on these sts working as given for Left Front to **.

Work rib for collar
Row 1: RS. Sl 1, rib 3, M1, k1, work 2tog, patt to end.
Row 2: Patt to last 6 sts, p1, M1, rib 4, k1b.
Complete as given for Left Front, reversing shapings.

SLEEVES (MAKE 2)
With 15 mm needles cast on 21 (21:23:23:25) sts and work 6 rows in rib as given for Back welt.
Cont in main patt placing patt as follows:
Row 1: RS. Knit.

Row 2: K1 (1:2:2:3), (p3, k5) twice, p3, k1 (1:2:2:3).
Row 3: P1 (1:2:2:3), (k3, p5) twice, k3, p1 (1:2:2:3).
Cont in patt as given for Back as now set, at the same time inc 1 st at both ends of the 13th (13th:7th:7th:7th) and 1 (1:2:2:3) foll 13th (13th:8th:8th:7th) rows. [25 (25:29:29:33) sts.]
Cont straight in patt until Sleeve measures 42 (42:42:44:44) cm (16½ (16½:16½:17½:17½) in) from beg, ending with a WS row.

Shape sleeve top
Cast off 5 (5:6:6:6) sts at beg of the next 2 rows, [15 (15:17:17:21) sts], 5 (5:6:6:7) sts at beg of the next 2 rows. Cast off rem 5 (5:5:5:7) sts.

BACK COLLAR
Join shoulders.
Next row: Beg at front edge st on Right Front Collar, sl 1, rib 12 (13:15:17:19), M1, knit up 9 (9:9:11:11) sts from back neck, starting at neck edge on Left Front Collar, M1, rib 12 (13:15:17:19), k1b. [37 (39:43:49:53) sts.]
Cont in rib until Back Collar measures 30 cm (11¾ in), ending with a WS row. Cast off ribwise.

POCKET BORDERS (MAKE 2)
With RS facing and 15 mm needles, rib across 11 sts from one pocket top. Rib 2 more rows. Cast off ribwise.

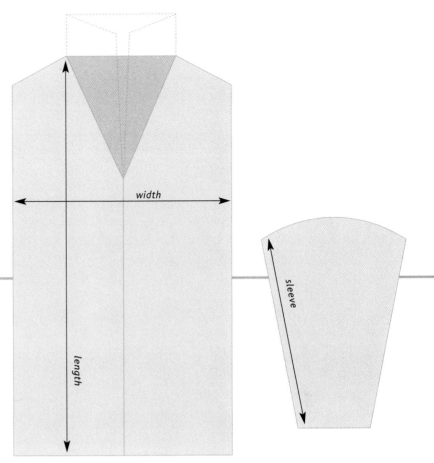

width

length

sleeve

TO MAKE UP

Sew pocket linings and borders in position.
Sew sleeves in position for approximately
21 (21:24:24:28) cm (8¼ (8¼:9½:9½:11) in)
from top of shoulder. Join side and sleeve seams.
For each tassel, cut 3 stands of yarn each
approximately 28 cm (11 in), see Making
Tassels, page 13. Tie in tassels to cast-off edge
on Collar approximately 4 sts apart. Trim as
required so that each tassel measures 12 cm
(4¾ in). Sew on buttons.
Cover with damp cloths and leave until dry.

HAT

With 15 mm needles, cast on 31 sts.
Row 1: RS. *P1, k1; rep from * to last st, p1.
Row 2: *K1, p1; rep from * to last st, k1.
Row 3: As row 1.
Inc row: K3, *M1, k2; rep from * 13 times,
M1, k2. [45 sts.]
Cont in patt as follows:
Row 1: RS. Knit.
Row 2: K5, *p3, k5; rep from * to end.
Row 3: P5, *k3, p5; rep from * to end.
Row 4: As Row 2.
Row 5: Knit.
Row 6: K1, *p3, k5; rep from * end last rep k1.
Row 7: P1, *k3, p5; rep from * end last rep p1.
Row 8: As Row 6.
Knit 2 rows.

Shape crown

Row 1 dec: RS. *Sl 1, k1, psso, k1, k2tog, k4;
rep from * 5 times. [35 sts.]
Purl 1 row.
Row 2 dec: *Sl 1, k1, psso, k1, k2tog, k2; rep
from * 5 times. [25 sts.]
Purl 1 row.
Row 3 dec: *Sl 1, k1, psso, k1, k2tog; rep
from * 5 times. [15 sts.]
Purl 1 row.
Row 4 dec: *K2tog; rep from * 7 times, k1.
[8 sts.]
Purl 1 row.
Row 5 dec: *K2tog; rep from * 4 times. [4 sts.]
Break yarn and thread through sts, pull up
tightly and secure.
Join back seam.
Make a tassel as given for Collar and tie in to
centre of crown (see Making Tassels, page 13).

This interesting yarn together with an easy slip stitch pattern gives extra appeal to this long line coat, which is perfect for wearing over a pair of casual trousers for a warm yet elegant look.

LONG SHAWL-COLLARED COAT

EASY

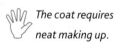

The slip stitch pattern used to make this coat is very easy to work.

Some experience is need to do the shaping and collar on this garment.

The coat requires neat making up.

MEASUREMENTS

To fit bust

81	86	91	97	102	cm
32	34	36	38	40	in

Actual width

95	100	104	113	117	cm
37½	39½	41	44½	46	in

Actual length

90	90	92	92	94	cm
35½	35½	36¼	36¼	37	in

Actual sleeve seam

46 cm

18 in

In the instructions figures are given for the smallest size first; larger sizes follow in brackets. Where only one set of figures is given this applies to all sizes.

MATERIALS

- 14 (14:15:15:16) × 100 g balls of Rowan Ribbon Twist in Ribble 111
- Pair of 12 mm needles
- Stitch holders
- 3 buttons

TENSION

9 sts and 11 rows to 10 cm (4 in) measured over pattern using 12 mm needles.

ABBREVIATIONS

See page 10.

COAT

BACK

With 12 mm needles cast on 51 (55:59:63:67) sts.

Foundation row: WS. *K3, p1; rep from * to last 3 sts, k3.

Row 1: *P3, k1 winding yarn twice round needle; rep from * to last 3 sts, p3.

Row 2: *K3, sl 1 purlwise wyif and dropping extra loop, yb; rep from * to last 3 sts, k3.

Rows 1 and 2 form the patt. Cont in patt dec 1 st at each end of the 17th and 5 (2:6:6:4) foll 8th (8th:6th:6th:6th) rows [39 (49:45:49:57) sts], then on the 0 (4:1:1:4) foll 0 (6th:4th:4th:4th) rows [39 (41:43:47:49) sts], then inc 1 st at each end of the next and foll 6th row.

[43 (45:47:51:53) sts.]

Work 10 rows straight, ending with a WS row.

[74 rows – work measures approximately 67 cm (26½ in) from beg.]

Shape armholes

Cast off 2 (2:3:3:4) sts at beg of the next 2 rows [39 (41:41:45:45) sts], then dec 1 st at each end of the next 3 rows [33 (35:35:39:39) sts], then on the 2 foll alt

rows [29 (31:31:35:35) sts]. Work a further 15 (15:17:17:19) patt rows, ending with a WS row.

Shape shoulders and back neck

Cast off 4 (4:4:5:5) sts at beg of the next row, work in patt until there are 5 (6:6:6:6) sts on RH needle after cast-off, turn and leave rem sts on a st holder. Work on these sts for first side.

Dec 1 st at neck edge on the next row. Cast off rem 4 (5:5:5:5) sts.

With RS facing, cast off the centre 11 (11:11:13:13) sts and work in patt to end. Complete this side to match first side, reversing shapings.

POCKET LININGS (MAKE 2)

With 12 mm needles cast on 11 sts. Cont in st st beg with a knit row. Work 14 rows and leave on a st holder.

LEFT FRONT

With 12 mm needles cast on 30 (34:36:38:40) sts.
Cont in patt as follows:

Foundation row: WS. (P1, k1) 3 times, p1, k3 (3:5:3:5), p1, *k3, p1; rep from * to last 3 sts, k3.

Row 1: *P3, k1 winding yarn twice round needle; rep from * to last 10 (10:12:10:12) sts, p3 (3:5:3:5), (k1, p1) 3 times, k1.

Row 2: (P1, k1) 3 times, p1, k3 (3:5:3:5), p1, *k3, sl 1 purlwise wyif and dropping extra loop, yb; rep from * to last 3 sts, k3.
Cont in patt as Back, dec 1 st at side edge on the 17th and 3 (2:4:4:4) foll 8th (8th:6th:6th:6th) rows [26 (31:31:33:35) sts], then on the 0 (2:0:0:1) foll 0 (6th:0:0:4th) rows [26 (29:31:33:34) sts]. Work 5 (1:5:5:1) rows, ending with WS row.

Place pocket

Next row: Patt 0 (0:2:2:0) tog, patt 4 (5:4:5:8) sts, rib across next 11 sts for pocket top, turn and work 2 rows in rib on these 11 sts, cast off these 11 sts. Break yarn. With RS facing, rejoin yarn to one pocket lining, cont in patt across these sts then patt 4 (6:7:7:8), rib 7. [26 (29:30:32:34) sts.]
Work 1 (3:5:5:1) rows. Dec 1 st at side edge on the next and 1 (1:1:1:2) foll 8th (6th:4th:4th:4th) row [24 (27:28:30:31) sts], then inc 1 st at side edge on the next and foll 6th row. [26 (29:30:32:33) sts.]
Work 4 rows straight, ending with a WS row. Place marker at front edge on last row. ***

Shape neck and collar

Row 1: Patt to last 10 sts, patt 3tog, M1, rib to end. [25 (28:29:31:32) sts.]
Row 2: Rib 8, patt to end.
Row 3: Patt to last 8 sts, M1, rib to end. [26 (29:30:32:33) sts.]

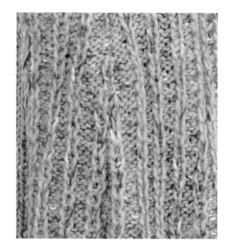

Row 4: Rib 9, patt to end.
Row 5: Patt to last 9 sts, M1, rib to end.
[27 (30:31:33:34) sts.]
Row 6: Rib 10, patt to end.

Shape armhole
Row 7: Cast off 2 (2:3:3:4) sts at beg of the next row, patt to last 13 sts, patt 3tog, M1, rib to end. [24 (27:27:29:29) sts.]
Row 8: Rib 11, patt to end.
Row 9: Patt 2tog, patt to last 11 sts, M1, rib to end. [24 (27:27:29:29) sts.]
Row 10: Rib 12, patt to last 2 sts, patt 2tog.
Row 11: Patt 2tog, patt to last 12 sts, M1, rib to end. [23 (26:26:28:28) sts.]
Row 12: Rib 13, patt to end.
1st size
Row 13: Patt 2tog, patt to last 13 sts, M1, rib to end. [23 sts.]
Row 14: Rib 14, patt to end.
2nd, 3rd, 4th and 5th sizes
Row 13: Patt 2tog, patt to last 16 sts, patt 3tog, M1, rib to end. [(24:24:26:26) sts.]
Row 14: Rib 14, patt to end.
All sizes
Row 15: Patt 2tog, patt to last 14 sts, M1, rib to end.
Rows 16, 18 and 20: In patt as set.
Row 17: Patt to last 15 sts, M1, rib to end.
Row 19: Patt to last 16 sts, M1, rib to end.
Row 21: Patt to last 17 sts, M1, rib to end. [26 (27:27:29:29) sts.]

3rd, 4th and 5th sizes
Row 22: In patt as set.
Row 23: Patt to last 18 sts, M1, rib to end. [(28:30:30) sts.]
5th size
Row 24: In patt as set.
Row 25: Patt to last 19 sts, M1, rib to end. [31 sts.]
All sizes
Work 9 rows as set, ending at side edge. [26 (27:28:30:31) sts.]

Shape shoulder
Cast off 4 (4:4:5:5) sts at beg of the next row, cast off 4 (5:5:5:5) sts on the foll alt row. [18 (18:19:20:21) sts.]
Next row: Rib 15 (15:16:17:18) sts, slip next st onto RH needle and take yarn to opposite side of work between needle, slip the same st back onto LH needle (referred to as wrap 1), turn.
Next row: In rib.
Next row: Rib 13 (13:14:15:16), wrap 1, turn.
Next row: In rib.
Next row: Rib 11 (11:12:13:14), wrap 1, turn.
Cont without shaping until collar is of sufficient length to go halfway across back of neck, ending with a WS row. Cast off.
Mark the positions of 3 buttons, the first in line with cast-off edge on pocket top, the last 4 rows down from marker and the remainder spaced between.

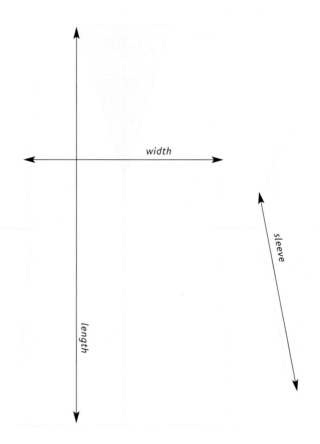

width

length

sleeve

RIGHT FRONT

With 12 mm needles cast on
30 (34:36:38:40) sts.
Cont in patt as follows:
Foundation row: *K3, p1; rep from * to last
10 (10:12:10:12) sts, k3 (3:5:3:5), (p1, k1)
3 times, p1.
Cont as now set, working as given for Left
Front reversing Place Pocket shapings to ***
and making buttonholes to correspond with
markers on left front as follows:
Buttonhole row 1: RS. Rib 3, cast off 1 st,
patt to end.
Buttonhole row 2: In patt, casting on 1 st
over st cast off on previous row.

Shape neck and collar

Row 1: Rib 7, M1, patt 3tog, patt to end.
Row 2: Patt to last 8 sts, rib to end.
Row 3: Rib 8, M1, patt to end.
Row 4: Patt to last 9 sts, rib to end.
Cont as now set, working as given for Left
Front, reversing shapings.

SLEEVES (MAKE 2)

With 12 mm needles cast on 19
(19:23:23:23) sts.
Cont in patt as given for Back, at the same
time inc 1 st at each end of the 5th and
1 (1:6:6:1) foll 4th (4th:6th:6th:4th) rows
[23 (23:37:37:27) sts], then on the 6 (6:0:0:6)
foll 6th rows. [35 (35:37:37:39) sts.]

Cont straight until Sleeve measures 46 cm
(18 in) from beg, ending with a WS row.

Shape sleeve top

Cast off 2 (2:3:3:4) sts at beg of the next
2 rows [31 sts], then dec 1 st at each end of
the next and 3 (3:5:5:6) foll alt rows
[23 (23:19:19:17) sts], then on the next
3 (3:1:1:0) rows. Cast off rem 17 sts.

TO MAKE UP

Join shoulders. Sew sleeve tops into armholes
then join side and sleeve seams.
Sew pocket linings in position. Sew ends of
collar together and sew in position at back of
neck. Sew on buttons.

This simple sweater is worked in easy stocking stitch – the easiest knitted fabric to create. Knitted in pretty pastel colours, it can be worn with trousers or a skirt.

STRIPED SWEATER

 *This garment is very easy to knit but take care not to pull the yarn too tight when carrying the colours up the side of the work.*

MEASUREMENTS

To fit bust

81	86	91	97	102	cm
32	34	36	38	40	in

Actual width

86	91	97	102	108	cm
34	36	38	40	42½	in

Actual length

53	53	54	55	56	cm
21	21	21¼	21½	22	in

Actual sleeve seam

46 cm

18 in

In the instructions figures are given for the smallest size first; larger sizes follow in brackets. Where only one set of figures is given this applies to all sizes.

MATERIALS

- 4 (5:5:6:7) × 50 g balls of Rowan Cotton Glace in Stout 814 (A)
- 3 (4:4:5:6) × 50 g balls of Rowan Cotton Glace in Pier 809 (B)
- 3 (3:3:4:4) × 50 g balls of Rowan Cotton Glace in Zeal 813 (C)
- 2 (2:2:3:3) × 50 g balls of Rowan Cotton Glace in Splendour 810 (D)
- Pair each of 3 mm and 3¾ mm needles
- Stitch holders

TENSION

22 sts and 30 rows to 10 cm (4 in) measured over stocking stitch using 3¾ mm needles.

ABBREVIATIONS

See page 10.

STRIPED SWEATER

Striped pattern

Work 8 rows in A, 6 rows in B, 4 rows in C, 2 rows in D, 4 rows in C, 6 rows in B, 8 rows in A, 2 rows in D, 2 rows in C, 2 rows in D. These 44 rows form the patt.

BACK

With 3 mm needles and A cast on 95 (101:107:113:119) sts and knit 9 rows. Change to 3¾ mm needles. Cont in st st beg with a knit row, working Stripe Sequence patt as above throughout, at the same time dec 1 st at each end of the 5th and 4 foll 5th rows. [85 (91:97:103:109) sts.]
Work 9 rows then inc 1 st at each end of the next and 4 foll 10th rows. [95 (101:107:113:119) sts.]
Work 19 rows, ending with a 6th patt row.

Shape armholes

Cast off 6 (7:8:8:9) sts at beg of the next 2 rows [83 (87:91:97:101) sts], then dec 1 st

at each end of the next row and 4 (4:5:6:7) foll
alt rows. [73 (77:79:83:85) sts.]
Work straight until armhole measures
19 (19:20:21:22) cm (7½ (7½:8:8¼:8½) in)
from beg of shaping, ending with a WS row.

Shape shoulders

Cast off 4 (5:5:5:5) sts at beg of the next
2 rows, 5 (5:5:5:6) sts on the foll 2 rows,
5 (5:5:6:6) on the foll 2 rows, 5 (5:6:6:6) on
the foll 2 rows. Leave rem 35 (37:37:39:39)
sts on a st holder for back neck.

FRONT

Work as given for Back until Front measures
18 rows shorter than Back to beg of shoulder
shaping, ending with a WS row.

Shape front neck

Knit 30 (31:32:33:34) sts, turn and leave
rem sts on a st holder. Work on these sts for
first side.
Dec 1 st at neck edge on the next 9 rows then
on the 2 foll alt rows. [19 (20:21:22:23) sts.]
Work 4 rows, ending with a WS row.

Shape shoulder

Cast off 4 (5:5:5:5) sts at beg of the next row,
5 (5:5:5:6) sts on the foll alt row, 5 (5:5:6:6)
sts on the foll alt row, work 1 row then cast off
rem 5 (5:6:6:6) sts.
With RS facing, slip the centre

13 (15:15:17:17) sts on a st holder, rejoin yarn and knit to end. Complete this side to match first side, reversing shapings.

SLEEVES (MAKE 2)

With 3 mm needles and A, cast on 44 (48:48:50:50) sts and knit 9 rows. Change to 3¾ mm needles.
Work 130 rows to armhole, in stripe sequence and sleeve shaping as follows:
6 rows in B, 4 rows in C, 2 rows in D, 4 rows in C, 6 rows in B, 8 rows in A, 2 rows in D, 2 rows in C, 2 rows in D, (work the 44 rows of stripe patt) twice, then cont in stripe patt work 6 rows in A, at the same time shape sleeve by inc 1 st at each end of the 5th and 2 (6:14:14:18) foll 6th rows, then on the 12 (9:3:3:0) foll 8th rows.
[74 (80:84:86:88) sts.]
Cont straight until all 130 rows are completed.

Shape sleeve top

Cast off 6 (7:8:8:9) sts at beg of the next 2 rows [62 (66:68:70:70) sts], then dec 1 st at each end of the next and 11 (10:13:13:17) foll alt rows [38 (44:40:42:34) sts], then at each end of the next 11 (13:11:11:7) rows. Cast off rem 16 (18:18:20:20) sts.

NECKBAND

Join left shoulder. With RS facing, 3 mm needles and A, knit across 35 (37:37:39:39) sts from back neck st holder, knit up 22 sts down left front neck, knit across 13 (15:15:17:17) sts from front neck st holder, knit up 22 sts up right front neck.
[92 (96:96:100:100) sts.]
Knit 9 rows. Cast off.

TO MAKE UP

Join right shoulder and neckband.
Sew sleeve tops into armholes then join side and sleeve seams.

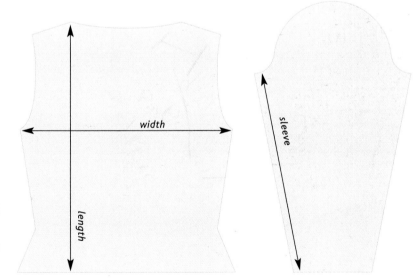

This smart cardigan with shawl collar worked in moss st and stripes is great for wearing with a simple pair of trousers. It has a loop stitch collar and ribbon tie.

CARDIGAN WITH LOOP STITCH COLLAR

★★☆ EASY

 *This cardigan is very easy to knit but the loop stitch collar takes a little more time to complete.*

MEASUREMENTS

To fit bust

81	86	91	97	102	107	cm
32	34	36	38	40	42	in

Actual width

89	94	99	104	109	114	cm
35	37	39	41	43	45	in

Actual length

58	60	61	62	64	66	cm
22¾	23¾	24	24½	25¼	26	in

Actual sleeve seam

43	46	46	46	46	47	cm
17	18	18	18	18	18½	in

In the instructions figures are given for the smallest size first; larger sizes follow in brackets. Where only one set of figures is given this applies to all sizes.

MATERIALS

- 8 (8:9:9:10:10) × 50 g balls of Rowan Summer Tweed in Storm 521 (A)
- 4 (4:4:5:5:5) × 50 g balls of Rowan Summer Tweed in Summer Berry 537 (B)
- 2 × 100 g balls of Rowan Yorkshire Tweed in Darkside 414 (C)
- Pair each of 4 mm and 5 mm needles
- 7 buttons
- Ribbon for front tie

TENSION

16 sts and 28 rows to 10 cm (4 in) measured over moss stitch using 5 mm needles.

ABBREVIATIONS

See page 10.

CARDIGAN

BACK

With 5 mm needles and A, cast on 71 (75:79:83:87:91) sts. Purl 2 rows.

Cont in moss st patt and stripe patt and shaping for sides as follows:

Rows 1 to 12: With A, *k1, p1; rep from * to last st, k1. (This row forms the moss st patt and is repeated throughout)

Row 13: As row 1, dec 1 st at each end of row. [69 (73:77:81:85:89) sts.]

Row 14: As row 1.

Rows 15 to 18: With C, work in moss st.

Row 19: With B, work as row 1, dec 1 st at each end of row. [67 (71:75:79:83:87) sts.]

Row 20: With B, work in moss st.

These 20 rows form the stripe patt (14 rows in A, 4 rows in C, 2 rows in B).

Cont in stripe patt throughout.

Work 4 rows in A, then cont to shape sides by dec 1 st at each end of the next and 2 foll 6th rows [61 (65:69:73:77:81) sts], then inc 1 st at each end of the foll 14th and 4 foll 10th rows. [71 (75:79:83:87:91) sts.]

Cont straight in patt until work measures 39 (41:41:41:42:43) cm (15½ (16:16:16:16½:17) in), ending with a WS row.

Shape armholes
Cast off 4 (4:5:5:6:6) sts at beg of the next 2 rows [63 (67:69:73:75:79) sts], then dec 1 st at each end of the next and 4 (4:4:5:5:6) foll alt rows. [53 (57:59:61:63:65) sts.] Cont straight in patt until armhole measures 19 (19:20:21:22:23) cm (7½ (7½:8:8¼:8¾:9) in), ending with a WS row.

Shape shoulders and back neck
Cast off 5 (5:6:6:6:6) sts at beg of the next row, patt to 13 (15:15:15:16:17) sts on RH needle after cast-off, turn and leave rem sts on a st holder. Work on these sts for first side. Work 3 rows, dec 1 st at neck edge on every row and casting off 5 (6:6:6:6:7) sts for shoulder on 2nd row. Cast off rem 5 (6:6:6:7:7) sts. With RS facing, rejoin yarn to rem sts and cast off centre 17 (17:17:19:19:19) sts, then patt to end. Complete this side to match first side, reversing shapings.

LEFT FRONT
With 5 mm needles and A, cast on 35 (37:39: 41:43:45) sts and purl 2 rows. Cont in moss st and stripe patt as Back. Work 12 rows then shape sides by dec 1 st at RH

edge on the next and 4 foll 6th rows [30 (32:34:36:38:40) sts], then inc 1 st at same edge on the foll 14th and 4 foll 10th rows. [35 (37:39:41:43:45) sts.] Work straight until Front matches Back to beg of armhole shaping, ending with the same patt row and at side edge.

Shape armhole and front edge
Cast off 4 (4:5:5:6:6) sts at beg of the next row. [31 (33:34:36:37:39) sts.] Work 1 row. Dec 1 st at each end of the next row. [29 (31:32:34:35:37) sts.] Work 8 (8:8:10:10:12) rows dec 1 st at armhole edge on the 4 (4:4:5:5:6) foll alt rows, and dec 1 st at front edge on the 2 (2:2:2:2:3) foll 4th rows. [23 (25:26:27:28:28) sts.] Keeping armhole edge straight work 24 (24:24:28:28:12) rows dec 1 st at front edge as set on every 4th row, then work 12 (12:12:12:12:30) rows dec 1 st on every foll 6th row. [15 (17:18:18:19:20) sts.] Cont straight in patt until Front measures the same as the Back to beg of shoulder shaping, ending at armhole edge.

Shape shoulder
Cast off 5 (5:6:6:6:6) sts at beg of the next row, 5 (6:6:6:6:7) sts on the foll alt row. Work 1 row. Cast off rem 5 (6:6:6:7:7) sts.

RIGHT FRONT

Work as given for Left Front, reversing shapings.

SLEEVES (MAKE 2)

With 5 mm needles and A, cast on
39 (39:41:41:43:43) sts. Purl 2 rows.
Cont in moss st and stripe patt as Back beg
with a 9th (7th:7th:7th:9th:11th) patt row.
Inc 1 st at each end of the 11th
(13th:9th:9th:9th:7th) row and 3 (7:3:3:10:1)
foll 12th (14th:10th:10th:10th:8th) row
[47 (55:49:49:65:47) sts.], then on the
4 (0:6:6:0:10) foll 14th (10th:12th:12th:0th:
10th) rows. [55 (55:61:61:65:67) sts.] Cont
straight in patt until Sleeve measures
43 (46:46:46:46:47) cm
(17 (18:18:18:18:18½) in) from beg, ending
with the same patt row as Back to beg of
armhole shaping.

Shape sleeve top

Cast off 4 (4:5:5:6:6) sts at beg of the next
2 rows. [47 (47:51:51:53:55) sts.] Dec 1 st at
each end of the next and 3 (3:4:4:3:3) foll alt
rows, then on the 4 (4:4:4:6:6) foll 4th rows,
then on the next 9 rows.
[13 (13:15:15:15:17) sts.] Cast off.

BUTTON BAND

With 4 mm needles and A, cast on 7 sts.
Row 1: RS. K2, (p1, k1) twice, k1.
Row 2: (K1, p1) 3 times, k1.

Rep these 2 rows until button band is long
enough to fit along left front edge to beg of
front edge shaping. Cast off in rib.
Sew to front edge then mark the positions of
7 buttons, the first to come 4 rows up from
cast-on edge, the last 4 rows down from cast-
off edge and the remainder spaced evenly
between.

BUTTONHOLE BAND

Work as given for Button band making
buttonholes to correspond with markers as
follows:
Buttonhole row 1: RS. Rib 3, cast off 1 st, rib
to end.
Buttonhole row 2: In rib, casting on over
cast-off st on previous row.

COLLAR

Join shoulders.

Left side

With 5 mm needles and B, cast on 5 sts.
Row 1: WS. Knit.
Row 2: K3, inc (by knitting and purling into
next st), k1, 6 sts.
Row 3: K1, inc in next st, k to end. [7 sts.]
Row 4: *K1 keeping st on LH needle bring yf,
pass yarn over left thumb to make a loop
(approximately 4 cm (1½ in), yb and knit this
st again, slipping st off the needle, yfon pass
the 2 sts just worked over this loop

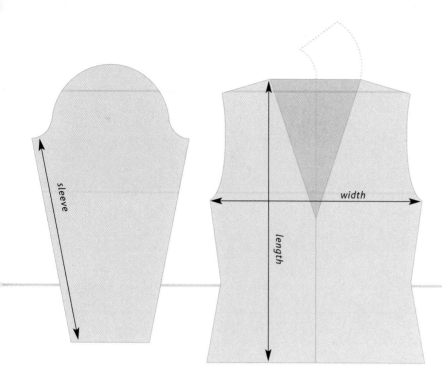

sleeve

width

length

(1 loop made); rep from * to last 2 sts, inc in next st, k1, 8 sts.

Row 5: As row 3. [9 sts.]

Row 6: As row 4. [10 sts.]

Rows 3 and 4 establish loop stitch patt. Cont in loop st patt throughout, inc 1 st at the same edge on the next and 1 (1:1:3:3:3) foll alt rows [12 (12:12:14:14:14) sts], then on the 6 foll 4th rows. [18 (18:18:20:20:20) sts.]

Cont straight, keeping the k2 at the shaped edge on each loop row, until collar is of sufficient length to go along shaped edge of front to shoulder, ending with a WS row. Place a marker at shaped edge on last row.

**Next row: Patt 16 (16:16:18:18:18), sl next st onto RH needle and take yarn to opposite side of work, between needles, sl same stitch back onto LH needle (referred to as Wrap 1), turn.

Next row: Knit.

Next row: Patt 14 (14:14:16:16:16), wrap 1, turn.

Next row: Knit.

Next row: Patt 11 (11:11:13:13:13), wrap 1, turn.

Next row: Knit.

Next row: Patt 8 (8:8:10:10:10), wrap 1, turn.

Next row: Knit.

Next row: Patt across all sts. **

Patt 11 more rows without shaping then rep from ** to ** once more.

Patt 4 more rows. Cast off loosely.

RIGHT SIDE

With 5 mm needles and B, cast on 5 sts.

Row 1: WS. Knit.

Row 2: K1, inc, k3. [6 sts.]

Row 3: Knit to last 2 sts, inc, k1. [7 sts.]

Row 4: K1, inc, work loop patt to end. [8 sts.]

Row 5: As row 3. [9 sts.]

Row 6: As row 4. [10 sts.]

Complete as given for Left Side, reversing shapings. Cast off loosely.

TO MAKE UP

Sew sleeve tops into armholes then join side and sleeve seams.

Join cast off edges of collar together then sew cast-on edges on collar to cast-off edges on front borders. Sew shaped edge on collar evenly around neck edges placing marker to shoulder seam.

Sew ribbon to seam under collar for approximately 3 cm (1¼ in) to secure.

Worn together or separately this set can be worn to be smart or casual with jeans. The jacket is knitted in moss stitch to give a lovely texture and the fringed edges, which are added after the knitting is complete, add extra style. The sleeveless top is created using a finer yarn in a two-colour slip stitch pattern and also has fringing round the neck.

MOSS STITCH JACKET AND TOP

HELPFUL HINTS
- Use a crochet hook or rug hook to help pull folded ends of tassels through work to speed up the process.

MEASUREMENTS
To fit bust

81	86	91	97	102	cm
32	34	36	38	40	in

JACKET
Actual width

87.5	93.5	100	106	109	cm
34½	37	39½	41¾	43	in

Actual length

58	60	61	62	64	cm
22¾	23¾	24	24½	25¼	in

Actual sleeve seam

43	46	46	46	46	cm
17	18	18	18	18	in

TOP
Actual width

81	89	97	101	105	cm
32	35	38	39¾	41¼	in

Actual length

52	53	54	55	56	cm
20½	21	21¼	21¾	22	in

In the instructions figures are given for the smallest size first; larger sizes follow in brackets. Where only one set of figures is given this applies to all sizes.

MATERIALS
For the jacket
- 6 (6:7:7:8) × 100 g balls of Sirdar Denim Chunky 567
- Pair of 6½ mm needles
- 2 buttons

For the top
- 2 (2:3:3:4) × 50 g balls of Sirdar Denim Tweed DK in Glacier 603 (A)
- 2 (2:3:3:4) × 50 g balls of Sirdar Denim Tweed DK in 567 (B)
- Pair each of 3¼ mm and 4 mm needles
- Stitch holders

TENSION

JACKET
13 sts and 22 rows to 10 cm (4 in) measured over moss stitch using 6½ mm needles.

TOP
20 sts and 32 rows to 10 cm (4 in) measured over pattern using 4 mm needles.

ABBREVIATIONS
See page 10.

 **EASY**

Some knitting experience is needed to complete the jacket shapings.

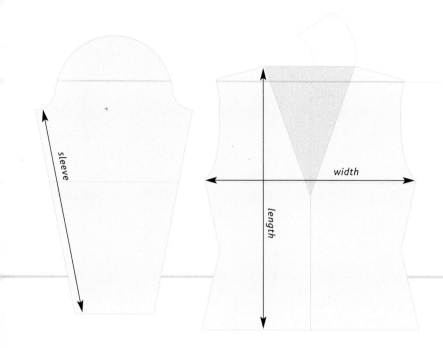

JACKET

BACK

With 6½ mm needles cast on 57 (61:65:69:71) sts. Cont in moss st as follows:

Row 1: *K1, p1; rep from * to last st, k1.
Rep this row throughout.
Shape sides by dec 1 st at each end of the 7th and 4 foll 8th rows [47 (51:55:59:61) sts], then inc 1 st at each end of the foll 8th and 4 foll 6th rows. [57 (61:65:69:71) sts.] Work straight until work measures 39 (41:41:41:42) cm (15½ (16:16:16:16½) in) from beg.

Shape armholes

Cast off 3 (3:4:5:5) sts at beg of the next 2 rows [51 (55:57:59:61) sts], then dec 1 st at each end of the 4 foll alt rows. [43 (47:49:51:53) sts.] Cont straight until armhole measures 19 (19:20:21:22) cm (7½ (7½:8:8¼:8¾) in) from beg of shaping.

Shape shoulders and back neck

Cast off 4 (4:5:4:5) sts at beg of the next row, patt until there are 11 (13:13:13:13) sts on RH needle, turn and work on these sts for first side. Work 3 rows dec 1 st at neck edge on every row and casting off 4 (5:5:5:5) sts for

shoulder on 2nd row. Cast off rem 4 (5:5:5:5) sts. Rejoin yarn and cast off centre 13 (13:13:17:17) sts, patt to end. Complete this side to match first side, reversing shapings.

LEFT FRONT

With 6½ mm needles cast on 33 (35:37:39:41) sts. Cont in moss st as Back, shaping sides by dec 1 st at RH edge on the 7th and 4 foll 8th rows [28 (30:32:34:36) sts], then inc 1 st at same edge on the foll 8th and 4 foll 6th rows. [33 (35:37:39:41) sts.] Work straight until Front measures the same as the Back to beg of armhole shaping, ending at side edge.

Shape armhole

Cast off 3 (3:4:5:5) sts at beg of the next row [30 (32:33:34:36) sts], dec 1 st at the same edge on the 4 foll alt rows. [26 (28:29:30:32) sts.] Cont straight until Front measures 13 rows shorter than Back to beg of shoulder shaping, ending at front edge.

COLLAR NOTCH

Cast off 5 sts in moss st patt, turn and cast on 5 sts, patt to end.
Cont in patt until Front measures the same as the Back to beg of shoulder shaping, ending at side edge.

Shape shoulder

Cast off 4 (4:5:4:5) sts at beg of the next row,

FRINGING FOR JACKET

For each tassel cut 2 lengths of yarn 7 cm (2¾ in) long, fold in half then tie in approximately 1.5 cm (¾ in) in from edge, spacing 1 cm (¼ in) apart (see page 13). Repeat all round collar edge, round outer edge on pockets, (not top pocket) and cuffs. Trim edges to neaten.

4 (5:5:5:5) sts on the 2 foll alt rows. Cont on the rem 14 (14:14:16:17) sts for collar to centre of back neck. Cast off in patt.
Mark the positions of 2 buttons, the first 14 cm (5½ in) and the second 24 cm (9½ in) up from cast-on edge.

RIGHT FRONT

Work as given for Left Front reversing shapings and working buttonholes at RH edge to correspond with markers.
Buttonhole row 1: Patt 3, (yo) twice, k2tog, patt to end.
Buttonhole row 2: In patt dropping one yo from previous row.

POCKETS (MAKE 2)

With 6½ mm needles cast on 11 sts. Cont in moss st. Work 1 row then inc 1 st at each end of the next 3 rows. [17 sts.] Cont straight until pocket measures 12 cm (4¾ in) from beg. Cast off in patt.

SLEEVES (MAKE 2)

With 6½ mm needles cast on 31 (31:33:33:35) sts and cont in moss st as Back, at the same time inc 1 st at each end of the 9th (11th: 11th:11th:7th) row and 1 (7:7:7:1) foll 10th (11th:11th:11th:8th) rows [35 (47:49:49:39) sts] then on the 5 (0:0:0:7) foll 12th (0:0:0:10th) rows. [45 (47:49:49:53) sts.] Cont straight until sleeve measures

43 (46:46:46:46) cm (17 (18:18:18:18) in) from beg.

Shape sleeve top

Cast off 3 (3:4:5:5) sts at beg of the next 2 rows [39 (41:41:39:43) sts], then dec 1 st at each end of the 5 (5:6:6:7) foll alt rows [29 (31:29:27:29) sts], then on the 2 foll 4th rows [25 (27:25:23:25) sts], then on the next 7 rows. Cast off rem 11 (13:11:9:11) sts in patt.

TO MAKE UP

Join shoulders. Join collar seam then sew to back of neck. Sew sleeve tops into armholes then join side and sleeve seams.
Sew pockets centrally on fronts positioning bottom of pocket 5 cm (2 in) up from cast-on edge. Sew on buttons. Add fringing (see left).

SLEEVELESS TOP

BACK AND FRONT (ALIKE)

With 3¼ mm needles and A, cast on 81 (89:97:101:105) sts. Work moss st border.
Row 1: *K1, p1; rep from * to last st, k1.
Rep this row 5 times more.
Change to 4 mm needles and cont in patt as follows:

Preparation rows:
Row 1: WS. With A, purl.
Row 2: With A, knit.

Row 3: With A, p2, *p1 wrapping yarn twice, p3; rep from * end last rep p2.
End of preparation rows.
Row 4: With B, k2, *sl 1 wyib dropping extra wrap, k1, insert needle into next st 2 rows below and draw through a loop loosely, knit next st and pass the loop over the st just knitted, k1; rep from * end sl 1 wyib, k2.
Row 5: With B, p2, *sl 1 wyif, p3; rep from * end sl 1 wyif, p2.
Row 6: With B, knit.
Row 7: With B, p2, *p1, wrapping yarn twice, p3; rep from * end last rep p2.
Rows 8 to 11: With A rep rows 4 to 7.
Rep rows 4 to 11 throughout.
Cont in patt until work measures 34 cm (13½ in) from beg, ending with a WS row.

Shape armholes

Cast off 6 (6:7:7:7) sts at beg of the next 2 rows [69 (77:83:87:91) sts], then dec 1 st at each end of the next 4 rows [61 (69:75:79:83) sts], then at each end of the 3 foll alt rows. [55 (63:69:73:77) sts.]
Cont straight until armhole measures 14 (15:16:17:18) cm (5½ (6 6¼:6¾:7) in) from beg of shaping, ending with a WS row.

Shape neck

Patt 13, turn and leave rem sts on a st holder. Work on these sts for first side. Patt 1 row. Work 11 rows dec 1 st at neck edge on every

row. [2 sts.] Cast off.
With RS facing, slip the centre 29 (37:43:47:51) sts on a st holder, rejoin yarn to rem 13 sts and patt to end. Complete this side to match first side, reversing shapings.

NECKBAND

Join left shoulder. With RS facing, 3¼ mm needles and A, knit up 12 sts along right back neck edge, knit across 29 (37:43:47:51) sts from back neck st holder, knit up 12 sts along left back neck, 12 sts along left front neck, knit across 29 (37:43:47:51) sts from front neck st holder, knit up 13 sts up right front neck. [107 (123:135:143:151) sts.]
Work 5 rows in moss st as welt. Cast off in moss st.

ARMBANDS (MAKE 2)

Join right shoulder and neckband.
With right side facing, 3¼ mm needles and A, knit up 91 (97:103:107:113) sts evenly along armhole edge. Work 5 rows in moss st as welt. Cast off in moss st.

TO MAKE UP

Join sides and armhole borders. Add fringing (see above right).

FRINGING FOR TOP

For each tassel cut 2 lengths of yarn A, 7 cm (2¾in) long, fold in half and tie in along first row worked for neckband approximately 1 cm (½ in) apart (see page 13). Repeat all round neckband. Trim edges to neaten.

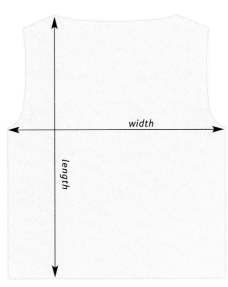

This 'wear anywhere' garment is something special. Knitted in a fabulous yarn which changes colour magically as you knit it has ribbed raglan sleeves and a lovely cosy high collar. The main body of jacket is knitted in easy stocking stitch

TWO-COLOUR JACKET

 **VERY EASY**

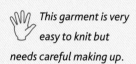 *This garment is very easy to knit but needs careful making up.*

MEASUREMENTS

To fit bust

81–86	91–97	102–107	cm
32–34	36–38	40–42	in

Actual width

94	105	113	cm
37	41¼	44½	in

Actual length

60	62	66	cm
23¾	24½	26	in

Actual sleeve seam

46	46	47	cm
18	18	18½	in

In the instructions figures are given for the smallest size first; larger sizes follow in brackets. Where only one set of figures is given this applies to all sizes.

MATERIALS

- 1 × 400 g ball of Sirdar Yo-Yo in 014
- Pair each of 3¾ mm and 4½ mm needles
- Stitch holders
- 7 buttons

TENSION

15 sts and 24 rows to 10 cm (4 in) measured over stocking stitch using 4½ mm needles.

ABBREVIATIONS

See page 10.

JACKET

BACK

Working from centre of ball, with 3¾ mm needles, cast on 75 (81:87) sts.

Row 1: RS. *K3, p3; rep from * to last 3 sts, k3.

Row 2: *P3, k3; rep from * to last 3 sts, p3.

Rep these 2 rows for 6 cm (2½ in) from beg, ending with a RS row.

Next row: Rib to end dec 4 (2:2) sts evenly across row. [71 (79:85) sts.]

Change to 4½ mm needles and cont in st st beg with a knit row.

Work 10 (10:14) rows. Work 19 rows dec 1 st at each end of the next and every foll 6th row. [63 (71:77) sts.] Work 11 rows without shaping.

Work 25 rows inc 1 st at each end of the next and every foll 8th row. [71 (79:85) sts.]

Cont without shaping until back measures 38 (38:40) cm (15 (15:15¾) in) from beg, ending with a WS row.

Shape raglans

Cast off 4 sts at beg of the next 2 rows. [63 (71:77) sts.]

Work 2 (4:4) rows dec 1 st at each end of every row. [59 (63:69) sts.]

Work 38 (40:46) rows dec 1 st at each end of the next and every foll alt row.

Cast off rem 21 (23:23) sts.

Shape raglan

Next row: Cast off 4 sts, knit to end.
[28 (32:35) sts.]
Next row: Purl.
Work 2 (4:4) rows dec 1 st at raglan edge on
every row. [26 (28:31) sts.]
Work 29 (31:33) rows dec 1 st at raglan edge on
the next and every foll alt row. [11 (12:14) sts.]

Shape neck

Next row: Cast off 3 (4:4) sts, purl to end.
[8 (8:10) sts.]
Work 2 rows dec 1 st at raglan edge on the
next row, at the same time dec 1 st at neck
edge on every row. [5 (5:7) sts.]
Work 5 (5:9) rows dec 1 st at raglan edge only
on next and every foll alt row. [2 sts.]
Next row: P2tog. Fasten off.

RIGHT FRONT

Working from outside of the ball, with 3¾ mm
needles cast on 39 (45:51) sts.
Work 2 rows in rib as given for Back welt.
Row 3: Rib 4, cast off 2 sts, rib to end.
Row 4: Rib to 4 sts, cast on 2 sts, rib 4.
Cont in rib for 6 cm (2½ in), ending with a
RS row.
Next row: Rib to last 9 sts, inc 2 sts evenly
across row for 1st size only and dec 3 sts across
row for 3rd size only, slip rem 9 sts onto a st
holder for Right Front border. [32 (36:39) sts.]
Change to 4½ mm needles and cont in st st.

LEFT FRONT

Working from outside of the ball, with 3¾ mm
needles cast on 39 (45:51) sts.
Work 6 cm (2½ in) in rib as given for Back
welt, ending with a RS row.
Next row: Rib 9, leave these 9 sts on a st holder
for Left Front border, rib to end inc 2 sts evenly
across row for 1st size only and dec 3 sts evenly
across row for 3rd size only. [32 (36:39) sts.]
Change to 4½ mm needles and cont in st st.
Work 10 (10:14) rows.
Work 19 rows dec 1 st at beg of the next and
every foll 6th row. [28 (32:35) sts.]
Work 11 rows without shaping.
Work 25 rows inc 1 st at beg of the next and
every foll 8th row. [32 (36:39) sts.]
Cont without shaping until left front measures
38 (38:40) cm (15 (15:15¾) in) from beg,
ending with a WS row.

Work 10 (10:14) rows. Work 19 rows dec 1 st end of the next and every foll 6th row. [28 (32:35) sts.]
Work 11 rows without shaping.
Work 25 rows inc 1 st at end of the next and every foll 8th row. [32 (36:39) sts.]
Cont without shaping until right front measures 38 (38:40) cm (15 (15:15¾) in) from beg, ending with a RS row.

Shape raglan
Next row: Cast off 4 sts, purl to end. [28 (32:35) sts.]
Work 2 (4:4) rows dec 1 st at raglan edge on every row. [26 (28:31) sts.]
Work 28 (30:32) rows dec 1 st at raglan edge on the next and every foll alt row. [12 (13:15) sts.]

Shape neck
Next row: Cast off 3 (4:4) sts, knit to last 2 sts, k2tog. [8 (8:10) sts.]
Next row: Purl.
Work 2 rows dec 1 st at neck edge on every row, at the same time dec 1 st at raglan edge on the next row. [5 (5:7) sts.]
Work 5 (5:9) rows dec 1 st at raglan edge only on the next and every foll alt row. [2 sts.]
Next row: P2tog. Fasten off.

LEFT SLEEVE
Working from the centre of the ball, with 3¾ mm needles cast on 33 sts.

Work in rib as given for Back welt for 6 cm (2½ in), ending with a WS row.
Change to 4½ mm needles and cont in rib as Back welt throughout, inc 1 st at each end of the 5th and every foll 8th (6th:2nd) row to 55 (43:39) sts, working inc sts in rib.
2nd and 3rd sizes only
Inc 1 st at each end of every foll (8th:6th) row to (57:63) sts, working inc sts in rib.
All sizes
Cont without shaping until sleeve measures 46 (46:47) cm (18 (18:18½) in) from beg, ending with a WS row.

Shape raglans
Cast off 4 sts at beg of the next 2 rows. [47 (49:55) sts.]
Work 12 (16:16) rows dec 1 st at each end of the next and every foll 4th row. [41 (41:47) sts.]
Work 28 (28:34) rows dec 1 st at each end of the next and every foll alt row.
Cast off rem 13 sts.

RIGHT SLEEVE
Working from outside of the ball work as given for Left Sleeve.

LEFT FRONT BAND
With RS facing and 3¾ mm needles, cast on 1 st (cast on st used to sew band to front), rib across 9 sts left on a st holder. [10 sts.]
Row 1: P3, k3, p3, k1.

HELPFUL HINT
Always knit to the recommended tension. Knit up a tension swatch before you start (see page 9) and make the necessary adjustments to achieve the correct tension. If you knit too loosely the stitches will rub against each other and cause pilling; if you knit too tightly the garment will be stiff and unpleasant to wear.

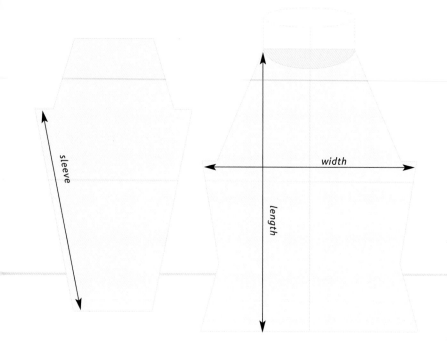

Row 2: P1, k3, p3, k3.

Rep these 2 rows until band is long enough to fit up front to beg of neck shaping, ending with a WS row. Break yarn and leave these sts on a st holder.

Mark the position of 6 buttons, the first to come 3 rows up from cast-on edge, the last 4 rows down from top and the remainder spaced evenly between.

RIGHT FRONT BAND

With WS facing and 3¾ mm needles, cast on 1 st (cast-on st used to sew band to front), rib across 9 sts left on st holder. [10 sts.]

Row 1: K3, p3, k3, p1.

Row 2: K1, p3, k3, p3.

Rep these 2 rows, working buttonhole rows as given for Right Front to correspond with markers on Left Front Border until band is long enough to fit up front to beg of neck shaping, ending with a WS row. Do not break off yarn.

NECKBAND

Join raglan seams.

With RS facing and 3¾ mm needles rib across 10 sts at top of Right Front Band as follows: k3, p3, k2, k2tog, knit up 11 (13:16) sts evenly along right side of neck, 13 sts evenly across top of left sleeve, 21 (23:23) sts evenly across back of neck, 13 sts evenly across top of right sleeve, 11 (13:16) sts evenly along left side of neck and work across 10 sts left on st holder at top of Left Front Band as follows: k2tog, k2, p3, k3. [87 (93:99) sts.]

Next row: Rib 9, p9 (9:10), inc in next st, (p9 (10:11), inc in next st) 5 times, p9 (10:10), rib 9. [93 (99:105) sts.]

Beg with a 1st row, work 18 rows in rib as given for Back welt.

Next row: Rib 4, cast off 2 sts, rib to end.

Next row: Rib to last 4 sts, cast on 2 sts, rib 4.

Work 3 rows in rib.

Cast off loosely in rib.

TO MAKE UP

Join side and sleeve seams. Sew front bands in position (using cast-on sts). Sew on buttons.

This easy-to-wear, cosy cape is knitted in two different colours and yarns which complement each other. Garter stitch ridges add extra texture.

TWO-COLOUR CAPE

MEASUREMENTS
To fit bust

81–91	97–107	cm
32–36	38–42	in

Actual length (excluding fringing)

58	60	cm
22¾	23¾	in

Actual width round lower edge

180	198	cm
71	78	in

In the instructions figures are given for the smallest size first; larger size follows in brackets. Where only one set of figures is given this applies to both sizes.

MATERIALS
- 3 (4) × 100 g balls of Rowan Plaid in Red 156 (A)
- 4 (5) × 100 g balls of Rowan Chunky Print in Black 079 (B)
- Pair each of 6 mm and 8 mm needles
- Stitch holders
- 2 buttons (1 large, 1 small)

TENSION
11½ sts and 15½ rows to 10 cm (4 in) measured over stocking stitch using 8 mm needles.

ABBREVIATIONS
See page 10.

CAPE

RIGHT SIDE (BACK AND FRONT WORKED IN ONE PIECE)
With 6 mm needles and A, cast on 104 (114) sts. Knit 4 rows.
Change to 8 mm needles. Cont in patt as follows:
Work 8 rows in st st, beg with a knit row.
Row 13 (dec row): K25 (28), sl 1, k1, psso, k50 (54), k2tog, k25 (28). [102 (112) sts.]
St st 5 more rows. Knit 4 rows.
Row 23 (dec row): K25 (28), sl 1, k1, psso, k48 (52), k2tog, k25 (28). [100 (110) sts.]
Knit 1 row.
Work 8 rows in st st.
Row 33 (dec row): K25 (28), sl 1, k1, psso, k46 (50), k2tog, k25 (28). [98 (108) sts.]
St st 5 more rows.
Cont in this way, working patt – 6 rows in g st and 14 rows in st st throughout, at the same time dec in the same way as before on the next and foll 6th row. [94 (104) sts.]
Then dec on the 3 foll 4th rows, then on the 18 (20) foll alt rows. [52 (58) sts.]
Work 1 row.
Next row: K25 (28), sl 1, k1, psso, k25 (28). [51 (57) sts.]
Next row: Purl.
Next row: K4, *k2tog, k5(2); rep from * 6 (12) times, k2tog, k3. [44 sts.]

This is a really straightforward and simple pattern which can be knitted up in a short amount of time.

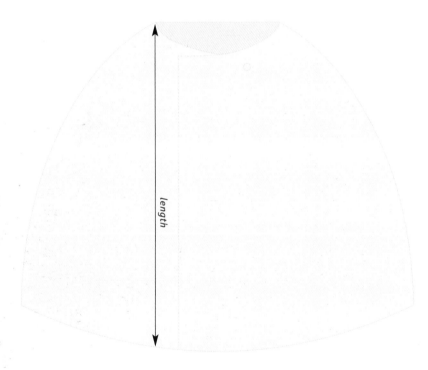

length

Next row: Purl and leave sts on a st holder.

LEFT SIDE (BACK AND FRONT WORKED IN ONE PIECE)

With 6 mm needles and B, cast on 104 (114) sts. Knit 4 rows.
Change to 8 mm needles and cont as given for Right Side.

TO MAKE UP

Join centre back seam.

NECKBAND

With RS facing and using 6 mm needles and B, knit across 43 sts from right side, k2tog, knit rem 43 sts from left side. [87 sts.] Knit 1 row. Cast off.

FRONT EDGES (MAKE 2)

With RS facing and using 6 mm needles and B, knit up 78 sts along one front edge. Knit 1 row. Cast off.

Sew the large button 12 cm (4¾ in) in from left front edge and the small button at the same distance on the wrong side on right front. Sew a loop on each top edge to correspond with buttons.
For each tassel cut 4 strands of yarn approximately 25 cm (9¾ in) long, tie in fringing evenly along lower edge (see Making Tassels, page 13). Work fringing in A on front worked in B, and in B on front worked in A.

WEEKEND

At the end of the week, it's time for relaxing and having fun and the garments in this chapter are perfect for lazy afternoons, strolls in the country and fun days out. Whether you want to just throw on a gorgeous poncho and hat knitted in a chunky soft yarn, or easy-to-wear hooded top or a knitted jacket with fashionable fur collar, there are plenty of designs in this chapter to suit every mood and style.

An easy-to-wear, cosy ribbed and cabled cardigan with hood. Cross stitches have been worked in a complementary colour to add that something different.

HOODED CARDIGAN WITH EMBROIDERY

★★☆ EASY

 *Some knitting skill is needed to create the cable pattern and cross stitch embroidery.*

Inserting the zip requires neat making up.

MEASUREMENTS
To fit bust

81–86	91–97	102–107	cm
32–34	36–38	40–42	in

Actual width

92.5	105	112.5	cm
36½	41¼	44¼	in

Actual length (from shoulder)
71 cm

28 in

Actual sleeve seam

44	46	47	cm
17¼	18	18½	in

In the instructions figures are given for the smallest size first; larger sizes follow in brackets. Where only one set of figures is given this applies to all sizes.

MATERIALS
- 11 (12:13) × 50 g balls of Rowan Cork 047
- 1 × 50 g ball of Rowan Handknit DK Cotton for embroidery in 313
- Pair each of 7 mm and 8 mm needles
- Cable needle
- Stitch holders
- 71 cm (28 in) open-ended zip

TENSION
16 sts and 19 rows to 10 cm (4 in) measured over pattern using 8 mm needles.

ABBREVIATIONS
C6 – slip 3 sts onto a cable needle and hold at front, k3 then k3 from cable needle.
See also page 10.

CARDIGAN

BACK
With 7 mm needles cast on 74 (84:90) sts.
1st and 3rd sizes
Row 1: RS. K1, p1, *k6, p2; rep from * to last 8 sts, k6, p1, k1.
Row 2: K2, *p6, k2; rep from * to end.
2nd size
Row 1: RS. K5, *p2, k6; rep from * to last 7 sts, p2, k5.
Row 2: K1, p4, *k2, p6; rep from * to last 7 sts, k2, p4, k1.
All sizes
Work a further 10 rows as now set.
Change to 8 mm needles. Cont in patt as follows:
1st size
Row 13: K1, p1, *C6, p2, k6, p2; rep from * to last 8 sts, C6, p1, k1.
Row 14: K2, *p6, k2; rep from * to end.
2nd size
Row 13: K5, *p2, C6, p2, k6; rep from * to last 15 sts, p2, C6, p2, k5.
Row 14: K1, p4, *k2, p6; rep from * to last 7 sts, k2, p4, k1.

CROSS STITCH

This can be worked singly (as here) or in blocks. Work a row of diagonal stitches from left to right and complete the crosses by working diagonal stitches back from right to left. Choose a nice contrast colour.

3rd size

Row 13: K1, p1, *k6, p2, C6, p2; rep from * to last 8 sts, k6, p1, k1.

Row 14: K2, *p6, k2; rep from * to end.

All sizes

Rows 15, 17, 19, 21 and 23: As row 1.

Rows 16, 18, 20, 22 and 24: As row 2.

Rep rows 13 to 24 throughout. Cont in patt until work measures 48 (46:44) cm (19 (18:17¼) in) from beg, ending with a WS row.

Shape raglans

Cast off 5 (6:7) sts at beg of the next 2 rows. [64 (72:76) sts.]

Next row: K2, k2tog, patt to the last 4 sts, k2tog-tbl, k2.

Next row: K1, p2, patt to last 3 sts, p2, k1.

Rep the last 2 rows 20 (22:24) times more, leave rem 22 (26:26) sts on a st holder.

LEFT FRONT

With 7 mm needles cast on 40 (45:48) sts.

1st and 3rd sizes

Row 1: RS. K1, p1, *k6, p2; rep from * to last 6 sts, (k1, p1) twice, k2.

Row 2: (K1, p1) 3 times, k2, *p6, k2; rep from * to end.

2nd size

Row 1: RS. K5, p2; *k6, p2; rep from * to last 6 sts, (k1, p1) twice, k2.

Row 2: (K1, p1) 3 times, k2, *p6, k2; rep from * to last 5 sts, p4, k1.

All sizes

Work a further 10 rows as now set. **

Change to 8 mm needles. Cont in patt as follows:

1st size

Row 13: K1, p1, *C6, p2, k6, p2; rep from * to last 6 sts, (k1, p1) twice, k2.

Row 14: (K1, p1) 3 times, k2, *p6, k2; rep from * to end.

2nd size

Row 13: K5, p2, *C6, p2, k6, p2; rep from * to last 6 sts, (k1, p1) twice, k2.

Row 14: (K1, p1) 3 times, k2, *p6, k2; rep from * to last 5 sts, p4, k1.

3rd size

Row 13: K1, p1, *k6, p2, C6, p2; rep from * to last 14 sts, k6, p2, (k1, p1) twice, k2.

Row 14: (K1, p1) 3 times, k2, *p6, k2; rep from * to end.

All sizes

Rows 15 to 24: As Back.

Cont in patt as given for Back until work measures same as Back to beg of raglan shaping, ending with a WS row (RS on right front).

Shape raglan

Cast off 5 (6:7) sts at beg of the next row. [35 (39:41) sts]. Work 1 row. (Omit this row on Right Front.)

Next row: K2, k2tog, patt to end.

Next row: Patt to last 3 sts, p2, k1.

Rep these 2 rows, 20 (22:24) times more.
[14 (16:16) sts.] Leave sts on a st holder.

RIGHT FRONT

Work as given for Left Front to **.
Change to 8 mm needles. Cont in patt as
follows:

1st size
Row 13: K2, (p1, k1) twice, *p2, k6, p2, C6;
rep from * to last 2 sts, p1, k1.

2nd size
Row 13: K2, (p1, k1) twice, p2, *k6, p2, C6,
p2; rep from * to last 5 sts, k5.

3rd size
Row 13: K2, (p1, k1) twice, p2; *k6, p2, C6,
p2; rep from * to last 8 sts, k6, p1, k1.
Cont as now set. Complete as given for Left
Front, reversing shapings, ending with a WS
row. Leave sts on a st holder.

SLEEVES (MAKE 2)

With 7 mm needles cast on 34 (38:42) sts.
Row 1: RS. P0 (0:2), k4 (6:6), *p2, k6; rep
from * to last 6 (8:10) sts, p2, k4 (6:6),
p0 (0:2).
Row 2: K0 (0, 2), p4 (6:6), k2, *p6, k2; rep
from * to last 4 (6:8) sts, p4 (6:6), k0 (0:2).
Work a further 10 rows as now set.
Change to 8 mm needles. **
Row 13: P0 (0:2), k4 (6:6), p2, C6, p2, k6,
p2, C6, p2, k4 (6:6), p0 (0:2).
Rep rows 13 to 24 as given for Back, at the

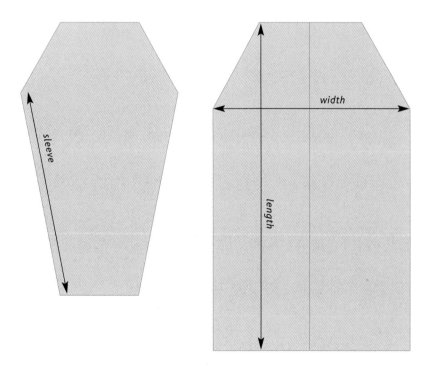

same time inc 1 st at each end of the foll 4th and 0 (0:1) foll 4th rows [36 (40:46) sts], then on the 9 (10:10) foll 6th rows [54 (60:66) sts], working patt into inc sts.

Cont straight until sleeve measures 44 (46:47) cm (17¼ (18:18½) in) from beg, ending with a WS row.

Shape raglans

Cast off 5 (6:7) sts at beg of the next 2 rows. [44 (48:52) sts.]

Row 1: K2, k2tog, patt to last 4 sts, k2tog-tbl, k2.

Rows 2 and 4: K1, p2, patt to last 3 sts, p2, k1.

Row 3: K3, patt to last 3 sts, k3.

Rep the last 4 rows, 4 times more [34 (38:42) sts], then dec 1 st at each end of the next and 10 (12:14) foll alt rows. [12 sts.]

Work 1 row. Leave sts on a st holder.

HOOD

Join raglans.

With right side facing and 8 mm needles, rib 6, k8 (10:10) sts from right front st holder, knit across 12 sts from top of right sleeve, work across 22 (26:26) sts from back neck as follows:

K6 (7:7), M1, (k5 (6:6), M1) twice, k6 (7:7), knit across 12 sts from top of left sleeve, then 8 (10:10) sts from left front, rib rem 6 sts as set. [77 (85:85) sts.]

Cont in st st beg with a purl row, keeping the 6 rib sts at each end on every row, until hood measures 35 cm (13¾ in) from beg, ending with a WS row. Cast off.

TO MAKE UP

Join hood seam. Join side and sleeve seams. Sew in zip. Make a tassel using 6 strands of yarn approximately 25 cm (10 in) long (see Making Tassels, page 13). Fold in half, wind yarn 1.5 cm (½ in) down from folded end and secure, thread yarn through loop formed and attach to point on back hood.

Work embroidered cross stitches on each rib between cables (see page 58).

Knitted with big yarn and big needles using stocking stitch, this tweedy jacket with funky fur collar could be worn anywhere.

JACKET WITH FUNKY COLLAR

MEASUREMENTS
To fit bust

81–86	91–97	102–107	cm
32–34	36–38	40–42	in

Actual width

100	110	120	cm
39½	43½	47¼	in

Actual length

57	59	61	cm
22½	23¼	24	in

Actual sleeve seam

46 cm

18 in

In the instructions figures are given for the smallest size first; larger sizes follow in brackets. Where only one set of figures is given this applies to all sizes.

MATERIALS
- 9 (10:11) × 100 g balls of Sirdar Bigga in 674 (A)
- 2 (3:3) × 50 g balls of Sirdar New Fizz in 0802 (B)
- Pair each of 12 mm and 15 mm needles
- Stitch holder
- 7 buttons

TENSION
6 sts and 9 rows to 10 cm (4 in) measured over stocking stitch using 15 mm needles.

ABBREVIATIONS
See page 10.

JACKET

BACK
With 12 mm needles and A, cast on 29 (33:35) sts.
Row 1: RS. *K1, p1; rep from * to last st, k1.
Row 2: *P1, k1; rep from * to last st, p1.
These 2 rows form the rib. Work 2 more rows in rib inc 1 (0:1) st in centre of last row. [30 (33:36) sts.]
Change to 15 mm needles. Cont in st st, beg with a knit row.
Work 4 rows.
Dec row: K1, k2tog, knit to last 3 sts, sl 1, k1, psso, k1.
Work 3 rows then work the dec row once more. [26 (29:32) sts.]
Work 7 rows straight.
Inc row: K1, M1, knit to last st, M1, k1. [28 (31:34) sts.]
Rep the last 8 rows once more. [30 (33:36) sts.]
Cont straight as now set until work measures 34 cm (13½ in) from beg, ending with a WS row.

Shape armholes
Cast off 2 (3:4) sts at beg of the next 2 rows [26 (27:28) sts], then dec 1 st at both ends of

★ ☆ ☆ **VERY EASY**

This garment is easy to knit but requires some care when picking up the stitches on each front edge.

the next and foll alt row. [22 (23:24) sts.] Cont straight in st st until armhole measures 23 (25:27) cm (9 (9¾:10¾) in), ending with a WS row.

Shape shoulders and back neck

Cast off 2 sts at beg of the next row, knit until there are 5 sts on RH needle, turn and leave rem sts on a st holder. Work on these sts for first side. Cast off 2 sts at neck edge, cast off rem 3 sts.

With RS facing, cast off the centre 8 (9:10) sts, k to end. Complete this side to match the first side, reversing shapings.

LEFT FRONT

With 12 mm needles and A, cast on 11 (13:13) sts and work 4 rows in rib as given for Back welt inc 1 (0:1) st in centre on last row. [12 (13:14) sts.]

Change to 15 mm needles. Cont in st st, beg with a knit row.

Work 4 rows.

Row 5 (dec): K1, k2tog, k to end.

Dec 1 st at RH edge on the foll 4th row. [10 (11:12) sts.]

Work 7 rows straight.

Next row: K1, M1, knit to end.

Rep the last 8 rows once more. [12 (13:14) sts.] Work straight as set until Front measures the same as the Back to beg of the armhole shaping, ending with a WS row.

Shape armhole

Cast off 2 (3:4) sts at beg of the next row. [10 sts.] Work 1 row.

Dec 1 st at armhole edge on the next and foll alt row. [8 sts.]

Cont straight until Front measures 5 rows shorter than Back to beg of right shoulder shaping, ending with a RS row.

Shape neck

Cast off 1 st at beg of the next row, then dec 1 st at neck edge on the next 2 rows. [5 sts.] Work 2 rows, ending at armhole edge.

Shape shoulder

Cast off 2 sts at beg of the next row. Work 1 row. Cast off rem 3 sts.

Mark the positions of 7 buttons, the first 2 rows up from cast-on edge and the last 2 rows down from the cast-off neck edge and the remainder spaced evenly between.

RIGHT FRONT

With 12 mm needles and A, cast on 21 (23:25) sts and work 4 rows in rib as given for Back welt inc 1 st in centre on last row. [22 (24:26) sts.]

Change to 15 mm needles. Cont in st st, beg with a knit row. Work 4 rows.

Row 5 (dec): Knit to last 3 sts, sl 1, k1, psso, k1. Dec 1 st at LH edge on the foll 4th row. [20 (22:24) sts.]

Work 7 rows.
Next row: Knit to last st, M1, k1.
Rep the last 8 rows once more.
[22 (24:26) sts.]
Cont until work measures the same as the Back to beg of armhole shaping, ending with a RS row.

Shape armhole

Cast off 2 (3:4) sts at beg of the next row.
[20 (21:22) sts.] Dec 1 st at armhole edge on the next and foll alt row.
[18 (19:20) sts.]
Cont straight until work measures 5 rows shorter than Back to left shoulder, ending at front edge.

Shape neck

Cast off 11 (12:13) sts at beg of the next row [7 sts], then dec 1 st at neck edge on the next 2 rows. [5 sts.]
Work 2 rows, ending at armhole edge.

Shape shoulder

Cast off 2 sts at beg of the next row. Work 1 row. Cast off rem 3 sts.

SLEEVES (MAKE 2)

With 12 mm needles and A, cast on 13 (15:17) sts and work 4 rows in rib as given for Back welt inc 1 st in centre on last row.
[14 (16:18) sts.]

Change to 15 mm needles. Cont in st st, beg with a knit row. Work 4 rows then inc 1 st at each end of the next and 4 foll 6th rows. [24 (26:28) sts.] Cont straight until sleeve measures 46 cm (18 in) from beg, ending with a WS row.

Shape sleeve top

Cast off 2 (3:4) sts at beg of the next 2 rows. [20 sts.]

Next row: K2tog, k to last 2 sts, sl 1, k1, psso. [18 sts.]

Dec 1 st at each end of the 0 (1:1) foll 4th rows. [18 (16:16) sts.] Dec 1 st at each end of the 3 (2:2) foll alt rows. [12 sts.]

Next row: WS. P2tog-tbl, purl to last 2 sts, p2tog. [10 sts.]

Work 3 more rows dec 1 st at each end of every row. [4 sts.] Cast off.

FRONT BANDS (MAKE 2)

With RS facing and using 12 mm needles and A, knit up 35 (36:37) sts along one front edge. Knit 1 row. Cast off.

COLLAR

Note: The purl side is the right side of the work. Join shoulders.

With 15 mm needles and B, cast on 106 (112:118) sts. Cont in st st until collar measures 21 cm (8¼ in) from beg. Cast off loosely.

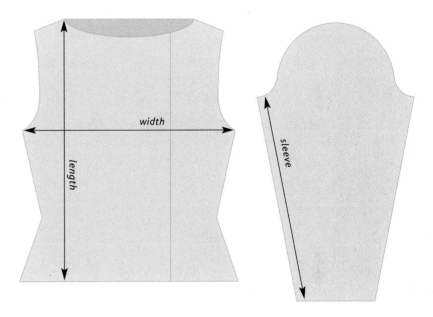

TO MAKE UP

Sew cast-on edge of collar to neck edge. Sew sleeve tops into armholes then join side and sleeve seams. Sew on buttons. Use natural holes in fabric for buttons to fasten.

PATCHWORK COAT

 *The stitch used in this garment (stocking stitch) is very simple to work.*

 *This project is slightly more challenging because of the number of colour changes.*

HELPFUL HINTS

- When working with different coloured yarns, use the Intarsia technique. Twist the new colour round the colour just used to link the colours together and avoid holes. Do not break off and join in except where absolutely necessary.

MEASUREMENTS

To fit bust

81–91	97–107	cm
32–36	38–42	in

Actual width

114	128	cm
45	50½	in

Actual length

94	99	cm
37	39	in

Actual sleeve seam (with cuff turned back)

41	42	cm
16	16½	in

In the instructions figures are given for the smallest size first; larger size follows in brackets. Where only one set of figures is given this applies to both sizes.

MATERIALS

- 4 (5) × 100 g balls of Sirdar Denim Chunky in Denim Blue Marl 516 (A)
- 3 (4) × 100 g balls of Sirdar Denim Chunky in Ivory Cream 508 (B)
- 2 (3) × 100 g balls of Sirdar Denim Chunky in Denim Blue 502 (C)
- 2 (3) × 100 g balls of Sirdar Denim Chunky in Camel 613 (D)
- Pair each of 5½ mm and 6½ mm needles
- 4 toggles

TENSION

14 sts and 19 rows to 10 cm (4 in) measured over stocking stitch using 6½ mm needles.

ABBREVIATIONS

See page 10.

COAT

BACK

With 5½ mm needles and A, cast on 78 (90) sts.

Row 1: RS. *K2, p2; rep from * to last 2 sts, k2.

Row 2: *P2, k2; rep from * to last 2 sts, p2.
These 2 rows form the 2x2 rib. Work 8 more rows in rib inc 2 (0) sts evenly on last row. [80 (90) sts.]
Change to 6½ mm needles. Cont in patt as follows:

Row 1: RS. K8 (9) A, k16 (18) B, k16 (18) C, k16 (18) D, k16 (18) B, k8 (9) A.

Row 2: P8 (9) A, p16 (18) B, p16 (18) D, p16 (18) C, p16 (18) B, p8 (9) A.

Rep these 2 rows 16 (17) times more.
[34 (36) patt rows.]

Row 35 (37): K8 (9) C, k16 (18) D, k16 (18)
B, k16 (18) A, k16 (18) D, k8 (9) C.

Row 36 (38): P8 (9) C, p16 (18) D, p16 (18)
A, p16 (18) B, p16 (18) D, p8 (9) C.

Rep these 2 rows 16 (17) times more.
[34 (36) patt rows.]

Rep rows 1 to 68 (72), then rows 1 to 34 (36)
once more. Cast off.

LEFT FRONT

With 5½ mm needles and A, cast on
38 (46) sts and work 10 rows in 2x2 rib as
given for Back welt inc 2 (dec 1) st evenly on
last row. [40 (45) sts.]

Change to 6½ mm needles. Cont in patt as
follows:

Row 1: RS. K8 (9) A, k16 (18) B, k16 (18) C.

Work a further 33 (35) rows as set.

Row 35 (37): K8 (9) C, k16 (18) D,
k16 (18) B.

Work a further 33 (35) rows as set.

Rep rows 1 to 34 (36) then rows 35 (37) to
52 (54) once, ending with a WS row.
[120 (126) rows.]

Shape front slope

Next row: Work in patt to the last 2 sts, sl 1,
k1, psso. Place a marker at end of row.

Patt 3 rows. Rep these 4 rows 6 (7) times
more, omitting markers. [33 (37) sts.]

Next row: Patt to the last 2 sts, sl 1, k1, psso.
Patt 5 rows. Rep these 6 rows once more.

Next row: Patt to last 2 sts, sl 1, k1, psso.
[30 (34) sts.]

Work 9 rows straight. Cast off.

RIGHT FRONT

With 5½ mm needles and A, cast on
38 (46) sts and work 10 rows in 2x2 rib as
given for Back welt inc 2 (dec 1) st evenly on
last row. [40 (45) sts.]

Change to 6½ mm needles. Cont in patt as
follows:

Row 1: Right side. K16 (18) D, k16 (18) B,
k8 (9) A.

Work a further 33 (35) rows as set.

Row 35 (37): K16 (18) A, k16 (18) D,
k8 (9) C.

Work a further 33 (35) rows as set.

Rep rows 1 to 34 (36) then rows 35 (37) to
52 (54) once, ending with a WS row.
[120 (126) rows.]

Shape front slope

Next row: Place a marker. K2tog, patt to end.
Complete as given for Left Front, reversing
shapings.

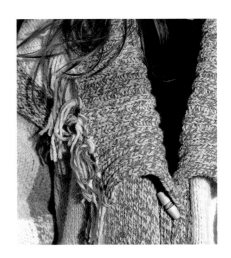

RIGHT SLEEVE

With 5½ mm needles and A, cast on
58 (62) sts and work 18 cm (7 in) in 2x2 rib as
given for Back welt ending with a WS row.
Dec row: Rib 1 (5), *rib 2tog, rib 4 (5); rep
from * 9 (7) times, rib 2tog, rib 1 (6).
[48 (54) sts.]
Change to 6½ mm needles. *** Cont in patt
as follows:
Row 1: RS. K8 (9) A, k16 (18) B, k16 (18) C,
k8 (9) D.
Cont as now set inc 1 st at each end of the
2 foll 4th rows [52 (58) sts], then on the 4 foll
6th rows. [60 (66) sts.] Work 1 (3) rows.
[34 (36) rows.]
Row 35 (37): K14 (15) C, k16 (18) D, k16
(18) B, k14 (15) A.
Cont as now set inc 1 st at each end of the foll
5th (3rd) and 3 foll 6th rows. [68 (74) sts.]
Work 3 (5) rows straight.

Shape top

Work 7 rows dec 1 st at each end of every row.
[54 (60) sts.] Cast off.

LEFT SLEEVE

Work as given for Right Sleeve to ***.
Cont in patt as follows:
Row 1: RS. K8 (9) D, k16 (18) C, k16 (18) B,
k8 (9) A.
Cont as now set inc 1 st at each end of the
2 foll 4th rows [52 (58) sts], then on the 4 foll
6th rows. [60 (66) sts.]
Work 1 (3) rows. [34 (36) rows.]
Row 35 (37): K14 (15) A, k16 (18) B, k16
(18) D, k14 (15) C.
Complete as given for Right Sleeve.

BUTTON BAND AND COLLAR

Join shoulders.
With 5½ mm needles and A, cast on 10 sts
and work in 2x2 rib as given for Back welt
until piece is long enough, when slightly
stretched, to fit up Left Front to marker **,
ending with a WS row. Mark end of last row
with a coloured thread.

Shape collar

Next row: Cast on 62 (66) sts, *p2, k2; rep
from * to end. Rep this row. [72 (76) sts.]
Cont in rib as set until Collar measures 8 cm
(3 in) from cast-on edge.
Change to 6½ mm needles and work a further
6 cm (2½ in) in rib as set. Cast off in rib.
Matching markers, sew Band to Left Front
then sew Collar neatly in place to centre back
of neck.
Mark the positions of 4 toggles on Band, the
first to come 28 (30.5) cm (11 (11¼ in) up
from cast-on edge and the last 2 cm (¾ in)
down from marker and the remainder spaced
evenly between.

BUTTONHOLE BAND AND COLLAR

Work as given for Button Band to **, ending with a RS row, marking end of last row with a coloured thread and working buttonholes to correspond with markers as follows:

Buttonhole row 1: RS. Rib 4, cast off next 2 sts, rib to end.

Buttonhole row 2: Rib, casting on over sts cast off on previous row.

Complete to match Button Band and Collar, working rib across all sts, *k2, p2; rep from * to end.

Matching markers, sew Band to Right Front then sew Collar neatly in place to centre back of neck. Join centre back seam of Collar.

TO MAKE UP

Mark depth of armhole 24 (26.5) cm (9½ (10½ in) from shoulder seam. Sew sleeve tops between markers then join side and sleeve seams, reversing seam on the last 9 cm (3½ in) for cuff. Sew on toggles.

For each tassel cut one 25 cm (9¾ in) length of each of the four colours.

Tie in tassels evenly spaced along collar edge (see Making Tassels, page 13).

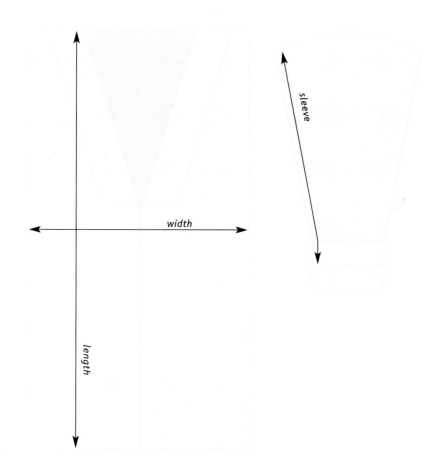

width

length

sleeve

This gorgeous poncho is so cosy. Knitted on the largest needles, the garment grows very quickly as you knit so although it is a large piece, it won't take you hours to complete. The tassels and large polo collar add a finishing touch – you won't want to take it off.

PONCHO AND HAT WITH EARFLAPS

HELPFUL HINTS

- The yarn alternates between thin, smooth threads and soft, furry nubs. While textured yarns can be difficult to knit, this one is easily knitted because the needle catches the smooth parts of the yarn neatly.
- You'll find that this garment grows quickly. Every time you work a row, you will be a centimetre closer to finishing!

MEASUREMENTS

To fit bust
86–102 cm
34–40 in
Actual length (without collar and fringes)
64 cm
25 in

MATERIALS

For the poncho
- 18 × 50 g balls of Rowan Big Wool Tuft in Frosty 055
- Pair each of 15 mm and 20 mm needles.

For the hat with earflaps
- 2 × 50 g balls of Rowan Big Wool Tuft in Frosty 055
- Pair of 20 mm needles

TENSION

5½ sts and 7 rows to 10 cm (4 in) measured over stocking stitch using 20 mm needles.

ABBREVIATIONS

See page 10.

PONCHO

BACK AND FRONT

With 15 mm needles cast on 79 sts. Purl 4 rows.
Change to 20 mm needles. Cont in st st beg with a knit row. Work 2 rows. Place a marker on the centre (40th) st.

Shape body

Row 1: K1, k2tog, knit to within 2 sts of marked st, k2tog-tbl, k2tog, knit to last 3 sts, k2tog-tbl, k1.
Row 2: Purl.
Row 3: Knit to within 2 sts of marked st, k2tog-tbl, k1, k2tog, knit to end.
Row 4: Purl.
Rep the last 4 rows, 9 times more. [19 sts.]
Cast off.

COLLAR

With RS facing and 15 mm needles, knit up 16 sts from front, then 16 sts from back. [32 sts.]

★☆☆☆ VERY EASY

VARIATION: HAT WITH BRIM

To make this hat you will need 2 × 50 g balls of Rowan Big Wool Tuft in Frosty 055. With 20 mm needles cast on 28 sts. Cont in st st beg with a knit row until the hat measures 20 cm (8 in) from beg, ending with a WS row.

Shape crown
Work as for hat with earflaps.

TO MAKE UP
Break yarn and thread through sts, pull up tightly and secure. Sew back seam, reversing seam on hat on the last 6 cm (2½ in) for brim. Press as instructions given on ball band.

Work in rev st st, beg with a purl row, for 10 cm (4 in). Change to 20 mm needles. Cont in rev st st until collar measures 20 cm (8 in) from beg. Knit 4 rows. Cast off loosely. Join left side and collar seam, reversing collar seam for turn-back. Along lower edge, tie in fringes that are about 12 cm (4¾ in) long, made with double yarn and spaced 3 sts apart.

TO MAKE UP
Press as instructions given on ball band. Join right seam.

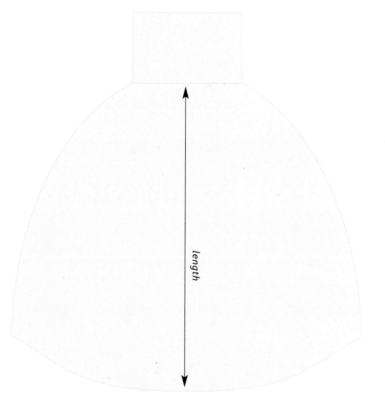

length

HAT WITH EARFLAPS

RIGHT EARFLAP
With 20 mm needles cast on 5 sts.
Cont in st st.
Row 1: Knit.
Row 2: Purl inc 1 st at both ends of row.
Row 3: Knit. **.
Row 4: Purl inc 1 st at end of row only. [8 sts.]
Work 2 rows and leave sts on a st holder.

LEFT EARFLAP
Work as given for Right Earflap side to **.
Row 4: Purl inc 1 st at beg of row only. [8 sts.]

BODY OF HAT
With 20 mm needles cast on 2 sts, knit across 8 sts from one ear flap, cast on 8 sts, knit across 8 sts from second ear flap, cast on 2 sts. [28 sts.]
Cont in st st beg with a purl row until main body of hat measures 15 cm (6 in) from cast-on edge, ending with a WS row.

Shape crown
Row 1: K1, (k2tog, k2) 6 times, k2tog, k1. [21 sts.]
Row 2: Purl.
Row 3: K1, (k2tog, k1) 6 times, k2tog. [14 sts.]
Row 4: Purl.
Row 5: (K2tog) 7 times. [7 sts.]

Watch the heads turn with envy when you wear this unusual pointed sweater with centre cable and fringing. If you prefer, you can add beads to the fringes – just make sure you choose ones with large holes.

SWEATER WITH FRINGING

★★☆ EASY

 *Some knitting skill is needed to create the cable design.*

The fringing requires neat and careful making up.

MEASUREMENTS

To fit bust

81–86	91–97	102–107	cm
32–34	36–38	40–42	in

Actual width

96	106	116	cm
37¾	41¾	45¾	in

Actual length (excluding fringing)

49	51	53	cm
19¼	20	20¾	in

Actual sleeve seam

43	46	46	cm
17	18	18	in

In the instructions figures are given for the smallest size first; larger sizes follow in brackets. Where only one set of figures is given this applies to all sizes.

MATERIALS

- 7 (8:9) × 100 g balls of Rowan Chunky Print in Girly Pink 077
- Pair each of 7 mm and 8 mm needles
- Stitch holders
- Cable needle

TENSION

12 sts and 15½ rows to 10 cm (4 in) measured over stocking stitch using 8 mm needles.

ABBREVIATIONS

C6 – slip next 3 sts to cable needle and hold at back, k3 then k3 from cable needle
See also page 10.

SWEATER

Cable pattern – worked over 6 sts
Rows 1 and 3: RS. Knit.
Rows 2 and 4: Purl.
Row 5: C6.
Rows 6 and 8: Purl.
Row 7: Knit.
These 8 rows form the patt and are repeated throughout.

BACK

With 8 mm needles cast on 6 sts.
Row 1: RS. Knit.
Row 2: Purl.
Row 3: Cast on 3 sts, k1, p2 on these 3 sts, k6.
Row 4: Cast on 3 sts, p1, k2 on these 3 sts, p6, k2, p1.
Row 5: Cast on 2 sts, k3, p2, C6, p2, k1.
Row 6: Cast on 2 sts, p3, k2, p6, k2, p3. [16 sts.]
Working the 8 row cable patt on the centre 6 sts, inc at sides as follows:
*Cast on 3 sts at beg of the next 2 rows then 2 sts on the foll 2 rows, working inc sts in st st
* rep from * to * 2 (3:3) more times.
[46 (56:56) sts.]

1st size

Cast on 3 sts at beg of the next 4 rows. [58 sts.]

2nd size

Cast on 4 sts at beg of the next 2 rows. [64 sts.]

3rd size

Cast on 3 sts at beg of the next 2 rows, cast on 4 sts at beg of the next 2 rows. [70 sts.]

All sizes

Cont as now set until side seam measures 30 cm (11¾ in) from end of shaping, ending with a WS row.

Shape armholes

Cast off 3 (4:5) sts at beg of the next 2 rows [52 (56:60) sts], then dec 1 st at each end of the next 3 rows [46 (50:54) sts], then on the 3 (3:4) alt rows. [40 (44:46) sts.] Cont straight until armhole measures 19 (21:23) cm (7½ (8¼:9) in) from beg of shaping, ending with a WS row.

Shape shoulders and back neck

Cast off 4 (5:5) sts at beg of the next row, knit until there are 8 sts on RH needle, turn and leave rem sts on a st holder. Work on these sts for first side.
Cast off 3 sts at neck edge on next row. Cast off rem 5 sts.
With RS facing, slip the centre 16 (18:20) sts on a st holder, rejoin yarn at neck edge and knit to end. Complete this side to match first side, reversing shapings.

FRONT

Work as given for Back until Front measures 16 rows shorter than Back to beg of shoulder shaping, ending with a WS row.

Shape neck

Next row: Knit until there are 14 (15:15) sts on RH needle, turn and leave rem sts on a st holder. Work on these sts for first side.
Work 10 rows dec 1 st at neck edge on every alt row. [9 (10:10) sts.]
Work 5 rows, ending with a WS row.

Shape shoulder

Cast off 4 (5:5) sts at beg of the next row.
Work 1 row. Cast off rem 5 sts.
Slip the centre 12 (14:16) sts on a st holder. Rejoin yarn and knit to end. Complete this side to match first side, reversing shapings.

SLEEVES (MAKE 2)

With 7 mm needles cast on 27 (29:31) sts and knit 4 rows inc 1 st in centre of last row. [28 (30:32) sts.]
Change to 8 mm needles. Cont in st st, beg with a knit row. Work 18 rows.
Inc 1 st at each end of the next and 2 (3:3) foll 12th (10th:10th) rows. [34 (38:40) sts.]
Cont straight until Sleeve measures 43 (46:46) cm (17 (18:18) in) from beg, ending with a WS row.

Shape sleeve top

Cast off 3 (4:4) sts at beg of the next 2 rows
[28 (30:32) sts], then dec 1 st at each end of
the next and 6 (7:8) foll alt rows [14 sts], then
on the next 3 rows. [8 sts.] Cast off.

LOWER EDGE (MAKE 2)

With 7 mm needles cast on 8 sts.

Row 1: K8.

Row 2: P4, k3, p1.

Rep these 2 rows until piece fits along lower
edge (do not stretch around point) ending
with a 2nd row.

Final row: Cast off 4 sts, draw yarn through
rem st on right hand needle, slip rem 3 sts off
needle and unravel them all the way down to
make fringe loops.

COLLAR

Join left shoulder.

With RS facing and 7 mm needles, knit
up 2 sts from right back neck, knit across
16 (18:20) sts from back neck st holder, knit
up 2 sts from left back neck, 15 sts down left
front neck, knit across 12 (14:16) sts from
front neck st holder, knit up 15 sts up right
front neck. [62 (66:70) sts.]

Cont in g st (every row knit) until collar
measures 14 cm (5½ in). Change to 8 mm
needles and cont in g st until collar measures
28 cm (11 in) from beg. Cast off loosely.

TO MAKE UP

Join right shoulder and collar reversing seam
on the last 15 cm (6 in). Sew sleeve tops into
armholes then join side and sleeve seams.
Sew edging to lower edges.

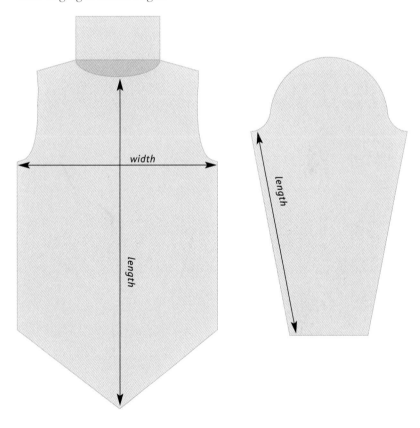

Knit in an evening! This stocking stitch wrap is knitted in a vibrant yarn for an eye-catching look.

THROW-OVER WRAP

★☆☆ VERY EASY

 *This project couldn't be simpler. The chunky yarn and large needles mean that it can be completed in a very short amount of time.*

MEASUREMENTS
Actual width
127 cm
50 in
Actual length (excluding fringing)
78 cm
30¾ in

MATERIALS
- 18 × 100 g balls of Rowan Biggy in 246
- Pair each of 15 mm and 20 mm needles

TENSION
5½ sts and 7 rows to 10 cm (4 in) measured over stocking stitch using 20 mm needles.

ABBREVIATIONS
See page 10.

WRAP

LEFT SIDE
With 15 mm needles cast on 32 sts.
Knit 5 rows for hem.
Next row: WS. K2, purl to last 2 sts, k2.
Next row: Knit.
These 2 rows form the patt and are repeated throughout. **
Cont in patt until work measures 78 cm (30¾ in) from beg, ending with a RS row.

Next row: Cast on 3 sts for back neck, knit across these 3 sts, k2 then purl to last 2 sts, k2. [35 sts.]
Next row: Knit.
Next row: Purl to last 2 sts, k2.
Rep the last 2 rows until back measures same as front to top of hem, ending with a RS row.
Knit 3 rows. Cast off knitwise.

RIGHT SIDE
Work as given for Left Side to **.
Cont in patt until work measures 78 cm (30¾ in) from beg, ending with a WS row.
Next row: Cast on 3 sts for back neck, purl across these 3 sts, purl 2, then knit to end. [35 sts.]
Next row: K2, purl to end.
Next row: Knit.
Rep the last 2 rows until back measures same as front to top of hem, ending with a RS row.
Knit 3 rows. Cast off knitwise.

TO MAKE UP
Join centre back seam neatly.
For each tassel cut 3 lengths of yarn each 25 cm (9¾ in) long and tie in evenly along lower edges (see Making Tassels, page 13).

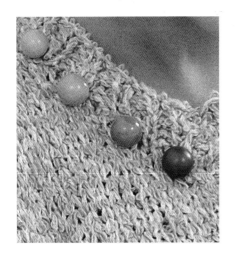

CASUAL

Casual elegance for everyday dressing, what could be easier to wear? These knitted cardigans, sweaters and tops are gorgeously cosy yet big on style, with simple stitch patterns and luxurious yarns. From the sweater with frilled edges in a textured cotton yarn to the striped sleeveless top worked in a chenille yarn with its velvety pile, these are all wonderfully easy to wear. All the patterns are easy to knit while some are ideal for the complete beginner – there is something here to suit everyone.

Dress up any garment with this cardigan worked in stocking stitch with a striped border pattern. The zigzag effect is created simply by increasing and decreasing at regular intervals. The cardigan is tied round the waist with ribbon and has coordinating ribbon on the cuffs.

CARDIGAN WITH RIBBON TIES

★★☆ EASY

The challenging part of this project is in the zigzag design.

MEASUREMENTS
To fit bust

81–86	91–97	102–107	cm
32–34	36–38	40–42	in

Actual width

91	102	113	cm
36	40	44½	in

Actual length (to lowest hem point)

62	65	68	cm
24½	25½	26¾	in

Actual sleeve seam (to lowest cuff point)

49	51	51	cm
19¼	20	20	in

In the instructions figures are given for the smallest size first; larger sizes follow in brackets. Where only one set of figures is given this applies to all sizes.

MATERIALS
- 10 (11:12) × 50 g balls of Rowan Wool Cotton in Poster Blue 948 (A)
- 1 × 50 g ball of Rowan Wool Cotton in Antique 900 (B)
- 1 × 50 g ball of Rowan Wool Cotton in French Navy 909 (C)
- Pair each of 3¼ mm and 4 mm needles
- Stitch holder
- Ribbon for waist and cuffs
- 9 buttons

TENSION
22 sts and 30 rows to 10 cm (4 in) measured over stocking stitch using 4 mm needles.

ABBREVIATIONS
See page 10.

CARDIGAN

BACK
With 4 mm needles and A, cast on 128 (146:164) sts and purl 3 rows.
Cont in patt as follows:
Row 1: WS. With A, purl.
Row 2: With A, k1, inc in next st (by knitting into front and back of st), k6, sl 1, k1, psso, k2tog, k6, *inc in each of next 2 sts, k6, sl 1, k1, psso, k2tog, k6; rep from * to last 2 sts, inc in next st, k1.
Row 3: With A, purl.
Row 4: As row 2.
Work 3 more rows in A, 4 rows in B, 2 rows in C, 2 rows in A as now set.
Row 16 (dec row): RS. With A, k1, inc in next st, k2, k2tog, k2, sl 1, k1, psso, (k2tog, k2) twice; *inc in each of next 2 sts, k2, k2tog, k2, sl 1, k1, psso, (k2tog, k2) twice; rep from * to last 2 sts, inc in next st, k1.
[114 (130:146) sts.]
Row 17 and 19: With A, purl.
Row 18: With A, k1, inc in next st, k5, sl 1, k1, psso, k2tog, k5, *inc in each of next 2 sts,

k5, sl 1, k1, psso, k2tog, k5; rep from * to last 2 sts, inc in next st, k1.

Work 3 more rows in A, 4 rows in B, 2 rows in C, 2 rows in A as now set.

Row 30 (dec row): RS. With A, k1, inc in next st, k1, k2tog, k2, sl 1, k1, psso, k2tog, k1, k2tog, k2, *inc in each of next 2 sts, k1, k2tog, k2, sl 1, k1, psso, k2tog, k1, k2tog, k2; rep from * to last 2 sts, inc in next st, k1. [100 (114:128) sts.]

Row 31: With A, purl.

Row 32: With A, k1, inc in next st, k4, sl 1, k1, psso, k2tog, k4, * inc in each of next 2 sts, k4, sl 1, k1, psso, k2tog, k4; rep from * to last 2 sts, inc in next st, k1.

Work 15 more rows in A as now set (47 patt rows have been worked).

Eyelet and dec row: With A, k1, (k2tog, yon) twice, [(k2tog, yon) twice, k3tog, yon] 12 (14:16) times, (k2tog, yon) 5 times, k1. [88 (100:112) sts.]

Next row: With A, purl.

Cont in st st and A, beg with a knit row, at the same time inc 1 st at each end of the foll 7th (7th:9th) and 5 foll 8th (9th:9th) rows [100 (112:124) sts], then cont straight until work measures 22 (23:24) cm (8½ (9:9½) in) from top of eyelet row, ending with a WS row.

Shape armholes

Cast off 6 (7:9) sts at beg of the next 2 rows [88 (98:106) sts], then dec 1 st at each end of the next 5 (5:7) rows, then on the 0 (2:2) foll alt rows. [78 (84:88) sts.] Cont straight until armhole measures 19 (21:23) cm (7½ (8¼:9) in) from beg of shaping, ending with a WS row.

Shape shoulders and back neck

Cast off 6 sts at beg of the next row, knit until there are 22 (24:25) sts on RH needle after cast off, turn and leave rem sts on a st holder. Work on these sts for the first side. Dec 1 st at neck edge on next row. Cast off 6 (6:7) sts for shoulder on next row and dec 1 st at neck edge. Dec 1 st at neck edge on next row. Cast off 6 (7:7) sts at shoulder on next row and dec 1 st at neck edge. Work 1 row. Cast off rem 6 (7:7) sts. With RS facing, rejoin yarn and cast off centre 22 (24:26) sts, knit to end. Complete this side to match the first side, reversing shapings.

LEFT FRONT

With 4 mm needles and A, cast on 65 (74:83) sts and purl 3 rows.

Cont in patt as follows:

1st and 3rd sizes

Row 1: WS. With A, purl.

Row 2: With A, k1, inc in next st, k6, sl 1, k1, psso, k2tog, k6, *inc in each of the next 2 sts, k6, sl 1, k1, psso, k2tog, k6; rep from * to last 11 sts, inc in each of the next 2 sts, k6, sl 1, k1, psso, k1.

2nd size

As given for Back.

All sizes

Cont as now set and in same stripe sequence as Back.

1st and 3rd sizes

Row 16 (dec row): Work in same way as given for Back to the last 11 sts, inc in each of next 2 sts, k2, k2tog, k2, sl 1, k1, psso, k1. [58 (74) sts.]

Row 30 (dec row): Work in same way as given for Back to the last 10 sts, inc in each of the next 2 sts, k1, k2tog, k2, sl 1, k1, psso, k1. [51 (65) sts.]

2nd size

Row 16 (dec row): Work in same way as given for Back to the last 2 sts, k2. [66 sts.]

Row 30 (dec row): Work in same way as given for Back to the last 2 sts, k2. [58 sts.]

All sizes

Cont until all 47 patt rows have been worked.

Eyelet and dec row: With A, k1, [(k2tog, yo) twice, k3tog, yo] 7 (8:9) times, k1. [44 (50:56) sts.]

Next row: With A, purl. Cont in st st and A beg with a knit row, inc 1 st at side edge on the 7th (7th:9th) and 5 foll 8th (9th:9th) rows [50 (56:62) sts], then work straight until Front measures same as Back to beg of armhole shaping, ending with a WS row.

Shape armhole and front edge

Cast off 6 (7:9) sts at beg of the next row, knit to the last 2 sts, k2tog. [43 (48:52) sts.] Purl 1 row. (Dec 1 st at each end of the next row, then 1 st at armhole edge on the next row) 2 (2:3) times. [37 (42:43) sts.] Dec 1 st at each end of the next row. [35 (40:41) sts.]

2nd and 3rd sizes

Dec 1 st at each end of the 2 foll alt rows. [36 (37) sts.]

All sizes

Keeping armhole edge straight, cont to dec 1 st at front edge on the 2 (0:0) foll alt rows, then the 9 (10:10) foll 4th rows [24 (26:27) sts], then work straight until Front measures same as Back to beg of shoulder shaping, ending with a WS row.

Shape shoulder

Cast off 6 sts at beg of the next row, 6 (6:7) sts on the foll alt row, 6 (7:7) sts on the foll alt row. Work 1 row. Cast off rem 6 (7:7) sts.

RIGHT FRONT

Work as given for Left Front placing patt as follows:

1st and 3rd sizes
Row 1: With A, purl.
Row 2: With A, k1, k2tog, k6, *inc in each of the next 2 sts, k6, sl 1, k1, psso, k2tog, k6; rep from * to last 2 sts, inc in next st, k1.
2nd size
Work as given for Back.
All sizes
Complete as given for Left Front, reversing shapings.

SLEEVES (MAKE 2)

With 4 mm needles and A, cast on 66 sts. Purl 3 rows.
Row 1: With A, purl.
Row 2: With A, k1, inc in next st, k5, sl 1, k1, psso, k2tog, k5, *inc in each of next 2 sts, k5, sl 1, k1, psso, k2tog, k5; rep from * to last 2 sts, inc in next st, k1.
Row 3: With A, purl.
Cont in patt as given for Back but in stripe sequence as follows:
Work 4 more rows in A, 4 rows in B, 2 rows in C, 2 rows in A.

Row 16 (dec row): With A, k1, inc in next st, k1, k2tog, k2, sl 1, k1, psso, k2tog, k2, k2tog, k1, *inc in each of next 2 sts, k1, k2tog, k2, sl 1, k1, psso, k2tog, k2, k2tog, k1; rep from * to last 2 sts, inc in next st, k1. [58 sts.]
Row 17: With A, purl.
Row 18: With A, k1, inc in next st, k4, sl 1, k1, psso, k2tog, k4, *inc in each of next 2 sts, k4, sl 1, k1, psso, k2tog, k4; rep from * to last 2 sts, inc in next st, k1.
Work 3 more rows in A, 4 rows in B, 2 rows in C, 3 rows in A.
Dec row: With A, p1 (3:3), *p2tog, p4 (5:8); rep from * 9 (7:5) times, p2tog, p1 (4:3). [48 (50:52) sts.]
Eyelet row: K2 (1:2), *k2tog, yon; rep from * to last 2 (1:2) sts, k2 (1:2).
Next row: With A, purl.
Cont in A and st st beg with a knit row, at the same time inc 1 st at each end of the 16 (17:19) foll 5th rows. [80 (84:90) sts.] Cont straight until sleeve measures 34 (36:36) cm (13½ (14:14) in) from top of eyelet row, ending with a WS row.

Shape sleeve top

Cast off 6 (7:9) sts at beg of the next 2 rows [68 (70:72) sts], then dec 1 st at each end of the next 10 rows [48 (50:52) sts], then on the 3 (4:5) foll 4th rows [42 (42:42) sts], then on the next 12 rows. [18 sts.] Cast off.

BUTTON BAND

With 3¼ mm needles and A, cast on 7 sts.
Cont in rib as follows:
Row 1: RS. K1, (k1b, p1) twice, k1b, k1.
Row 2: K1, (p1, k1b) 3 times.
Cont in rib as set until band (when slightly
stretched) fits up left front to beg of front
edge shaping, ending with a 2nd rib row.

Shape collar

Rib 3, k1, p1 into back of loop between st just
knitted and next st, rib to end.
Work 3 rows without inc.
Rep the last 4 rows until there are 37 sts
ending at straight edge (opposite side to incs).
Cast off 10 sts, return st on RH needle to LH
needle, recast on 10 sts using cable method
(insert RH needle between first two sts on LH
needle, yon, place loop onto LH needle).
Cont without further shaping until collar fits
to centre of back neck. Cast off ribwise.
Sl st into place.
Place markers for buttons, the first 2 cm
(¾ in) up from cast-on edge the last 2 cm
(¾ in) down from beg of front edge shaping
and the remainder spaced evenly between.

BUTTONHOLE BAND

Work as given for Button Band making
buttonholes to correspond with markers on
Button Band as follows:-
Row 1: RS. Rib 3, (yon) twice, k2tog-tbl, rib 2.

Row 2: Rib across row dropping one of the
(yon) loops.
Complete as given for Button Band.

Shape collar

Rib to last 3 sts, p1 and k1 into back of loop
between st just knitted and next st, p1, k1b,
k1. [9 sts.]

TO MAKE UP

Press as instructions on ball band.
Join shoulders. Join collar seam at centre of
back neck then sew to back neck. Sew sleeve
tops into armholes then join side and sleeve
seams. Thread ribbon through eyelet holes on
waist and sleeves.

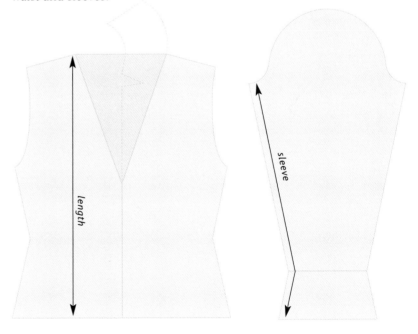

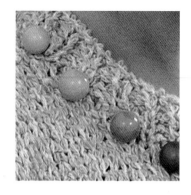

This cardigan is worked in an unusual ribbon yarn and using a simple stocking stitch, which is very easy to work and creates a fabric in no time. The beads round the neckline make this a really pretty garment.

CARDIGAN WITH BEADS

🖐 *Stocking stitch is one of the easiest knitted fabrics to create.*

MEASUREMENTS
To fit bust

81	86	91	97	102	107	cm
32	34	36	38	40	42	in

Actual width

85	91	97	102	108	114	cm
33½	36	38	40	42½	45	in

Actual length

58	60	61	62	64	66	cm
22¾	23¾	24	24½	25¼	26	in

Actual sleeve seam

43	46	46	46	46	47	cm
17	18	18	18	18	18½	in

In the instructions figures are given for the smallest size first; larger sizes follow in brackets. Where only one set of figures is given this applies to all sizes.

MATERIALS
- 11 (12:13:14:15:16) × 50 g balls of Rowan Cotton Braid in 352
- Pair each of 7 mm and 8 mm needles
- Stitch holders
- Large beads for decoration round neck
- 7 buttons for fastening

TENSION
10½ sts and 17 rows to 10 cm (4 in) measured over stocking stitch using 8 mm needles.

ABBREVIATIONS
See page 10.

CARDIGAN

BACK
With 7 mm needles cast on 45 (47:51:54:57:59) sts.
Row 1: RS. *K1, p1; rep from * to last st, k1.
Row 2: *P1, k1; rep from * to last st, p1.
Rep these 2 rows 2 times more inc 0 (1:0:0:0:1) sts in centre on last row. [45 (48:51:54:57:60) sts.]
Change to 8 mm needles. Cont in st st beg with a knit row shaping sides by dec 1 st at each end of the 5th and 3 foll 6th rows, then inc 1 st at each end of the foll 8th and 3 foll 6th rows. [45 (48:51:54:57:60) sts.] Cont straight until work measures 39 (41:41:41:42:43) cm (15½ (16:16:16:16½:17) in) from beg, ending with a WS row.

Shape armholes
Cast off 3 (3:4:4:5:5) sts at beg of the next 2 rows [39 (42:43:46:47:50) sts], then dec 1 st at each end of the 2 (2:2:3:3:3) foll alt rows. [35 (38:39:40:41:44) sts.] Cont straight until armhole measures 19 (19:20:21:22:23) cm [7½ (7½:8:8¼:8¾:9) in] from beg of shaping, ending with a WS row.

Plain knitted sweaters and cardigans look wonderful when embellished wtih interesting buttons, beads, ribbons, sequins or embroidery.

Shape shoulders and back neck

Cast off 3 (4:4:4:4:4) sts at beg of the next row, knit until there are 11 (11:11:11:12:13) sts on right hand needle after cast off, turn and work on these sts for first side. Leave rem sts on a st holder.

Work 3 rows dec 1 st at neck edge on each row and casting off 4 (4:4:4:4:5) sts for shoulder on the 2nd row. Cast off rem 4 (4:4:4:5:5) sts.

With RS facing, leave the centre 7 (8:9:10:9:10) sts on a st holder, rejoin yarn and knit rem 14 (15:15:15:16:17) sts. Complete this side to match first side, reversing shapings.

LEFT FRONT

With 7 mm needles cast on 21 (23:25:27:27:29) sts and work 6 rows in rib as given for Back welt inc 1 (1:0:0:1:1) sts in centre on last row. [22 (24:25:27:28:30) sts.]

Change to 8 mm needles. Cont in st st beg with a knit row shaping side by dec 1 st at RH edge on the 5th and 3 foll 6th rows [18 (20:21:23:24:26) sts], then inc 1 st at same edge on the foll 8th and 3 foll 6th rows. [22 (24:25:27:28:30) sts.]

Cont straight until Front measures same as Back to beg of armhole shaping, ending with a WS row.

Shape armhole

Cast off 3 (3:4:4:5:5) sts at beg of the next row [19 (21:21:23:23:25) sts], then dec 1 st at same edge on the 2 (2:2:3:3:3) foll alt rows. [17 (19:19:20:20:22) sts.] Cont straight until work measures 13 rows shorter than Back to beg of shoulder shaping, ending with a RS row.

Shape neck

Cast off 3 (4:4:5:4:5) sts at beg of the next row [14 (15:15:15:16:17) sts], then dec 1 st at neck edge on the 3 foll alt rows. Work 6 rows straight ending at armhole edge. [11 (12:12:12:13:14) sts.]

Shape shoulder

Cast off 3 (4:4:4:4:4) sts at beg of the next row, 4 (4:4:4:4:5) sts on the foll alt row. Work 1 row. Cast off rem 4 (4:4:4:5:5) sts.

RIGHT FRONT

Work as given for Left Front, reversing shapings.

SLEEVES (MAKE 2)

With 7 mm needles cast on 21 (21:23:23:25:25) sts and work 6 rows in rib as given for Back welt.

Change to 8 mm needles. Cont in st st beg with a knit row, at the same time inc 1 st at each end of the 7th (5th:5th:5th:5th:5th) row and 6 (1:1:1:5:7) foll 8th (6th:6th:6th:6th:6th) rows [35 (25:27:27:37:41) sts], then on the

0 (6:6:6:3:2) foll 0th (8th:8th:8th:8th:8th) rows. [35 (37:39:39:43:45) sts.] Cont straight until Sleeve measures 43 (46:46:46:46:47) cm (17 (18:18:18:18:18½) in) from beg, ending with a WS row.

Shape sleeve top

Cast off 3 (3:4:4:5:5) sts at beg of the next 2 rows [29 (31:31:31:33:35) sts], then dec 1 st at each end of the next and 7 (7:8:8:9:9) foll alt rows [13 (15:13:13:13:15) sts], then on the next 3 rows. [7 (9:7:7:7:9) sts.] Cast off.

NECKBAND

Join shoulders.

With RS facing and 7 mm needles, knit up 17 (18:18:19:19:20) sts from right front neck edge, 3 sts from right back neck, working across st holder for back neck, k7 (8:9:10:9: 10) sts from back neck dec 0 (1:0:1:0:1) sts in centre of these sts, knit up 3 sts from left back neck and 17 (18:18:19:19:20) sts down left front neck. [47 (49:51:53:53:55) sts.]

Work 5 rows in rib as given for back welt. Cast off in rib.

BUTTON BAND

With 7 mm needles cast on 6 sts and cont in rib as follows:

Row 1: RS. Sl 1, (k1, p1) twice, k1b.

Rep this row until band fits up left front to top of neckband. Cast off in rib. Sew in place.

Mark the position of 7 buttons, the first 1.5 cm (¾ in) up from cast-on edge, the last 1.5cm (¾ in) down from top of neckband and the remainder spaced evenly between.

BUTTONHOLE BAND

With 7 mm needles cast on 6 sts and cont in rib as button band making buttonholes to correspond with markers as follows:

Buttonhole row 1: RS. Sl 1, k1, cast off next st, rib to end.

Buttonhole row 2: In rib casting on over cast of st on previous row.

TO MAKE UP

Sew sleeve heads into armholes then join side and sleeve seams. Sew on buttons. Sew on beads.

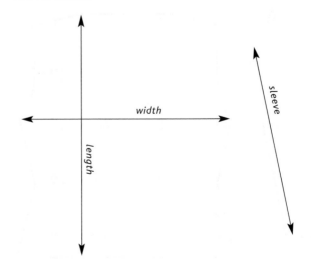

This lovely sweater is knitted using a textured yarn and has a panel of knit/purl diagonal stitches on the front and back. The bell edging detail on the cuffs and lower hem make this a pretty, feminine sweater.

SWEATER WITH FRILLED HEM AND CUFFS

 ★★☆ EASY

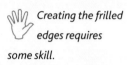 *Creating the frilled edges requires some skill.*

The diagonal stitch pattern requires concentration.

MEASUREMENTS
To fit bust

81	86	91	97	102	cm
32	34	36	38	40	in

Actual width

88	93	98	103	108	cm
34¾	36¾	38½	40½	42½	in

Actual length

53	53	54	55	56	cm
21	21	21¼	21¾	22	in

Actual sleeve seam

44	47	47	47	47	cm
17½	18½	18½	18½	18½	in

In the instructions figures are given for the smallest size first; larger sizes follow in brackets. Where only one set of figures is given this applies to all sizes.

MATERIALS
- 9 (9:10:10:11) × 50 g hanks of Rowan Summer Tweed in 508
- Pair of 5 mm needles
- Stitch holders

TENSION
16 sts and 23 rows to 10 cm (4 in) measured over stocking stitch using 5 mm needles.

ABBREVIATIONS
See page 10.

SWEATER

BACK AND FRONT (ALIKE)
With 5 mm needles cast on 207 (219:231:243:255) sts and work bell edge patt as follows:

Rows 1 and 3: RS. P3, *k9, p3; rep from * to end.

Rows 2 and 4: K3, *p9, k3; rep from * to end.

Row 5: P3, *yb, sl 1, k1, psso, k5, k2tog, p3; rep from * to end.

Rows 6 and 8: K3, *p7, k3; rep from * to end.

Row 7: P3, *k7, p3; rep from * to end.

Row 9: P3, *yb, sl 1, k1, psso, k3, k2tog, p3; rep from * to end.

Rows 10 and 12: K3, *p5, k3; rep from * to end.

Row 11: P3, *k5, p3; rep from * to end.

Row 13: P3, *yb, sl 1, k1, psso, k1, k2tog, p3; rep from * to end.

Rows 14 and 16: K3, *p3, k3; rep from * to end.

Row 15: P3, *k3, p3; rep from * to end.

Row 17: P3, *yb, sl 1, k2tog, psso, p3; rep from * to end.

Row 18: K3, *p1, k3; rep from * to end.
These 18 rows form the bell edge.
[71 (75:79:83:87) sts.]

Cont as follows:

Row 1: K19 (21:23:25:27), p1, k1b, (p2, k2) 7 times, p1, k1b, p1, k19 (21:23:25:27).

Row 2: P19 (21:23:25:27), k1, p1, k2, (p2, k2) 6 times, p2, k1, p1, k1, p19 (21:23:25:27).

Row 3: K19 (21:23:25:27), p1, k1b, (k2, p2) 7 times, k1, k1b, p1, k19 (21:23:25:27).

Row 4: P19 (21:23:25:27), k1, p3, (k2, p2) 7 times, k1, p19 (21:23:25:27).

These 4 rows form the patt. Cont in patt until work measures 34 cm (13½ in) from beg, ending with a WS row.

Shape armholes

Cast off 3 (3:4:4:5) sts at beg of the next 2 rows [65 (69:71:75:77) sts], then dec 1 st at each end of the 5 (5:6:6:7) foll alt rows. [55 (59:59:63:63) sts.]

Cont straight in patt until armhole measures 15 (15:16:17:18) cm (6 (6:6¼:6½:7) in) from beg of shaping, ending with a WS row.

Shape neck

K18 (19:19:20:20), turn and leave rem sts on a st holder, work on these sts for first side. Work 10 rows, dec 1 st at neck edge on every row. Work 1 row. Cast off rem 8 (9:9:10:10) sts.

With RS facing, slip the centre 19 (21:21:23:23) sts on a st holder, rejoin yarn and patt to end. Complete this side to match first side, reversing shapings.

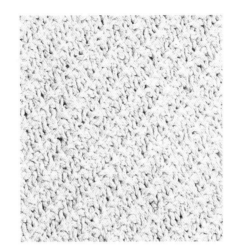

SLEEVES (MAKE 2)

With 5 mm needles cast on 87 (87:99:99:111) sts and work the 18 rows of bell edge as given for Back. [31 (31:35:35:39) sts.]

Cont in st st beg with a knit row, at the same time inc 1 st at each end of the 3rd and 3 foll 4th rows [39 (39:43:43:47) sts], then on the 8 (9:9:9:9) foll 8th rows. [55 (57:61:61:65) sts.] Cont straight until sleeve measures 44 (47:47:47:47) cm (17½ (18½:18½:18½:18½) in) from beg, ending with a WS row.

Shape sleeve top

Cast off 3 (3:4:4:5) sts at beg of the next 2 rows [49 (51:53:53:55) sts], then dec 1 st at each end of the next and 8 (7:8:8:11) foll alt rows [31 (35:35:35:31) sts], then on the next 9 (11:11:11:9) rows. Cast off rem 13 sts.

NECKBAND

Join left shoulder.

With 5 mm needles, knit up 9 sts down right back neck, knit across 19 (21:21:23:23) sts from st holder, knit up 9 sts up left back neck, 9 sts down left front neck, knit across 19 (21:21:23:23) sts from st holder, knit up 9 sts up right front neck.

[74 (78:78:82:82) sts.] Knit 1 row. Cast off.

TO MAKE UP

Join right shoulder.
Sew sleeve tops into armholes then join side and sleeve seams.

HELPFUL HINT

When measuring your work, lay the pieces out on a flat surface and smooth out, without stretching. This will guarantee accurate measurements.

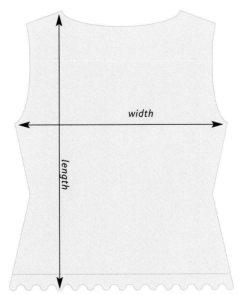

width

length

sleeve

Knitted in a chunky yarn this three-quarter-sleeved top is knitted in stocking stitch with a pretty leaf and bobble border. The lace-effect detail round the neck and the ribbon tie is a delightful added touch.

SCOOP-NECKED TOP WITH LACY EDGING

MEASUREMENTS
To fit bust

81	86	91	97	102	107	cm
32	34	36	38	40	42	in

Actual width

82	85	92	98	105	111	cm
32¼	33½	36¼	38½	41½	43¾	in

Actual length

56	57	58	59	59	61	cm
22	22½	22¾	23¼	23¼	24	in

Actual sleeve seam

25	27	27	27	28	28	cm
9¾	10¾	10¾	10¾	11	11	in

In the instructions figures are given for the smallest size first; larger sizes follow in brackets. Where only one set of figures is given this applies to all sizes.

MATERIALS
- 4 (4:5:5:6:6) × 100 g balls of Sirdar Denim Chunky in Lilac Frost 564
- Pair each of 5½ mm and 6½ mm needles
- 5½ mm circular needle
- Stitch holder
- Ribbon

TENSION
14 sts and 19 rows to 10 cm (4 in) measured over stocking stitch using 6½ needles.

ABBREVIATIONS
MB – Make bobble: (k1,yo,k1,yo,k1) into one st, turn, p5, turn, k5, turn, p1, p3tog, p1, turn, sl 1, k2tog, psso, completing bobble. *See also page 10.*

SWEATER

BACK
Using 6½ mm needles cast on 58 (60:65:69:74:78) sts.
Work 4 rows in st st beg with a knit row.
Leaf patterned border
Row 1: RS. K3 (4:3:5:4:6), p1; *MB, p1, k4, p1, rep from * to last 5 (6:5:7:6:8) sts, MB, p1, k3 (4:3:5:4:6).
Row 2: Purl, working p1b in top of MB.
Row 3: K3 (4:3:5:4:6), p1; *(k1, yo, k1) in next st, p1, k4, p1, rep from * to last 5 (6:5:7:6:8) sts, (k1, yo, k1) in next st, p1, k3 (4:3:5:4:6).
Row 4 and all other WS rows: Work sts as they appear on needle.
Row 5: K3 (4:3:5:4:6), p1, *k1, (k1, yo, k1) in next st, k1, p1, k4, p1; rep from * to last 7 (8:7:9:8:10) sts, k1, (k1, yo, k1) in next st, k1, p1, k3 (4:3:5:4:6).
Row 7: K3 (4:3:5:4:6), p1, *k2, (k1, yo, k1) in next st, k2, p1, k4, p1; rep from * to last 9 (10:9:11:10:12) sts, k2, (k1, yo, k1) in next st, k2, p1, k3 (4:3:5:4:6).

Row 9: K3 (4:3:5:4:6), p1, *k7, p1, k4, p1; rep from * to last 11 (12:11:13:12:14) sts, k7, p1, k3 (4:3:5:4:6).

Row 11: K3 (4:3:5:4:6), p1, *sl 1, k1, psso, k3, k2tog, p1, k4, p1; rep from * to last 11 (12:11:13:12:14) sts, sl 1, k1, psso, k3, k2tog, p1, k3 (4:3:5:4:6).

Row 13: K3 (4:3:5:4:6), p1, *sl 1, k1, psso, k1, k2tog, p1, k4, p1; rep from * to last 9 (10:9:11:10:12) sts, sl 1, k1, psso, k1, k2tog, p1, k3 (4:3:5:4:6).

Row 15: K3 (4:3:5:4:6), p1, *sl 1, k2tog, psso, p1, k4, p1; rep from * to last 7 (8:7:9:8:10) sts, sl 1, k2tog, psso, p1, k3 (4:3:5:4:6).

Row 16: As Row 4.

Cont in st st beg with a knit row until work measures 30 (30:30:31:31:31) cm (12 (12:12:12¼:12¼:12¼) in) from beg, ending with a WS row. **

Shape raglan

Cast off 3 (3:3:3:4:4) sts at beg of the next 2 rows. [52 (54:59:63:66:70) sts.]

1st, 2nd, 3rd and 4th sizes only

Work 12 (12:8:4) rows dec 1 st at both ends of the next and every foll 4th (4th:4th:0th) row. [46 (48:55:61) sts.]

All sizes

Work 12 (14:20:24:28:32) rows dec 1 st at both ends of the next and every foll alt row, 34 (34:35:37:38:38) sts. Cast off rem sts.

FRONT

Work as given for Back to **.

Shape raglan

Cast off 3 (3:3:3:4:4) sts at beg of the next 2 rows. [52 (54:59:63:66:70) sts.]

1st, 2nd, 3rd and 4th sizes only

Work 12 (12:8:4) rows dec 1 st at both ends of the next and every foll 4th (4th:4th:0th) row. [46 (48:55:61) sts.]

All sizes

Work 4 (6:12:16:20:24) rows dec 1 st at both ends of the next and every foll alt row. [42 (42:43:45:46:46) sts.]

Shape neck

Next row: K2tog, k7, turn and leave rem 33 (33:34:36:37:37) sts on a st holder. Working on these 8 sts only proceed as follows:

Next row: Purl.

Work 5 rows dec 1 st at both ends of the next and every foll alt row. [2 sts.]

Next row: P2tog.

Fasten off.

With RS facing, rejoin yarn to rem 33 (33:34:36:37:37) sts, cast off 24 (24:25:27:28:28) sts, knit to last 2 sts, k2tog. [8 sts.] Complete to match first side of neck.

SLEEVES (MAKE 2)

Using 5½ mm needles cast on 38 (38:42:42:46:46) sts, work 5 cm (2 in) in

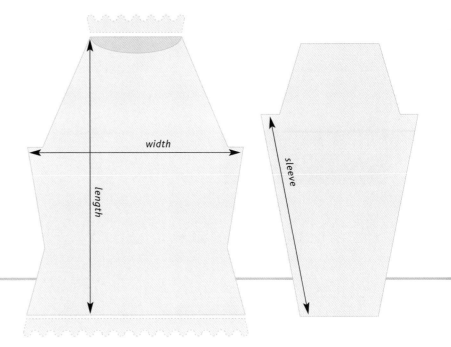

rib as follows, ending with a WS row:

Row 1: RS. *K2, p2; rep from * to last
2 sts, k2.

Row 2: *P2, k2; rep from * to last 2 sts, p2.
Change to 6½ mm needles. Cont in st st beg
with a knit row, inc 1 st at both ends of the 5th
and every foll 6th (6th:6th:6th:7th:7th) row to
50 (50:54:54:58:58) sts.

Cont without shaping until sleeve measures
25 (27:27:27:28:28) cm
(9¾ (10¾:10¾:10¾:11:11) in) or length
required, ending with a WS row.

Shape raglan

Cast off 3 (3:3:3:4:4) sts at beg of the next
2 rows. [44 (44:48:48:50:50) sts.]
Work 8 (12:8:8:4:12) rows dec 1 st at both
ends of the next and every foll 4th (4th:4th:
4th:0th:4th) row. [40 (38:44:44:48:44) sts.]
Work 16 (14:20:20:24:20) rows dec 1 st at
both ends of the next and every foll alt row.
Cast off rem 24 sts.

NECKBAND

With 5½ mm needles and using the thumb
method, cast on 211
(211:211:222:222:222) sts.

Row 1: RS. Purl.

Row 2: K2, *k1, slip this st back onto LH
needle, lift the next 8 sts on LH needle over
this st and off needle, (yf) twice, knit the first
st again, k2; rep from * to end.

Row 3: K1, *p2tog, drop loop of 2 sts made in
previous row and (k1, k1b) twice, into it, p1;
rep from * to last st, k1. ***
[116 (116:116:122:122:122) sts.]
Knit 2 rows.

Eyelet row: K4 (4:4:2:2:2), * yf, k2tog, k2; rep
from * to end.
Purl 3 rows. Cast off knitwise.

LOWER BORDER

With 5½ mm circular needle and using the
thumb method, cast on 211
(222:233:244:255:266) sts and work as given
for Neckband to ***.
[116 (122:128:134:140:146) sts.]
Knit 4 rows. Cast off knitwise.

TO MAKE UP

Join raglans then side and sleeve seams.
Beginning at centre back, sew Neckband to
neck edge and Lower Border to lower edge
beginning at side seam. Join short ends.
Thread ribbon in and out of eyelets on
neckband and tie in a bow at centre of front
neck. Pin out garment to the measurement
given on page 96. Cover with damp cloths and
leave until dry.

Keep the chill off with this simple V-necked slipover. It is made using a chenille yarn to give a luxurious look and is worked in stocking stitch with subtle striped colour changes.

STRIPED SLEEVELESS TOP

★★☆ EASY

 *This simple garment requires some skill when it comes to picking up stitches for the armholes.*

MEASUREMENTS

To fit bust

81	86	91	97	102	cm
32	34	36	38	40	in

Actual width

81	86	91	97	102	cm
32	34	36	38	40	in

Actual length

55	56	57	58	59	cm
21½	22	22½	23	23¼	in

In the instructions figures are given for the smallest size first; larger sizes follow in brackets. Where only one set of figures is given this applies to all sizes.

MATERIALS

- 2 (2:2:3:3) × 100 g balls of Rowan Chunky Cotton Chenille in Angel Tears 391 (A)
- 1 (1:1:2:2) × 100 g balls of Rowan Chunky Cotton Chenille in Flutter 389 (B)
- 1 (1:1:2:2) × 100 g balls of Rowan Chunky Cotton Chenille in Wraith 394 (C)
- Pair each of 4 mm and 5 mm needles
- Stitch holder
- Safety pin

TENSION

15 sts and 26 rows to 10 cm (4 in) measured over stocking stitch using 5 mm needles.

ABBREVIATIONS

2tog-tbl – work 2 stitches together through back of loops
See also page 10.

SLEEVELESS TOP

BACK

With 4 mm needles and A, cast on 61 (65:69:73:77) sts.
Row 1: RS *k1, p1; rep from * to last st, k1.
Row 2: *P1, k1; rep from * to last st, p1.
These 2 rows form the rib; work 4 more rows in rib.

Change to 5 mm needles. Cont in st st beg with a knit row and stripe patt, at the same time, shaping for sides as given below:
Stripe sequence: Work 6 rows in A, 4 rows in B, (2 rows in A, 2 rows in C), twice, 2 rows in A, 4 rows in B. These 24 rows form the patt and are repeated throughout. Cont in patt dec 1 st at both ends of the 5th and 4 foll 4th rows [51 (55:59:63:67) sts], then inc 1 st at both ends of the foll 12th and 4 foll 8th rows. [61 (65:69:73:77) sts.]
Cont straight in patt until work measures 35 cm (13¾ in) from beg, ending with a WS row. **

Shape armholes

Cast off 4 (4:5:5:6) sts at beg of the next 2 rows [53 (57:59:63:65) sts], then dec 1 st at both ends of the next 4 rows [45 (49:51:55:57) sts], then on the 3 foll alt rows. [39 (43:45:49:51) sts.]

Cont straight in patt until armhole measures 20 (21:22:23:24) cm (8 (8¼:8½:9:9½) in) from beg, ending with a WS row.

Shape shoulders and back of neck

Cast off 3 (4:4:5:5) sts at beg of the next row, knit until there are 8 (9:9:10:10) sts on RH needle after cast-off. Work on these sts for first side. Cast off 4 sts at neck edge on next row. Cast off rem 4 (5:5:6:6) sts.

With RS facing, slip the centre 17 (17:19:19:21) sts on a st holder, rejoin yarn and knit to end. Complete as given for first side, reversing shapings.

FRONT

Work as given for Back to **.

Shape armholes and divide for V-neck

Cast off 4 (4:5:5:6) sts at beg of the next row, knit until there are 26 (28:29:31:32) sts on RH needle after cast-off. Turn and work on these sts for first side.

Dec 1 st at beg of the next row. Work 10 rows dec 1 st at neck edge on the 2 foll 4th rows, at the same time, dec 1 st at armhole edge on the next 4 rows and 3 foll alt rows. [16 (18:19:21:22) sts.]

Keeping armhole edge straight, cont to dec 1 st at neck edge on every 4th row to 7 (9:9:11:11) sts, then work straight until Front matches Back to beg of shoulder shaping, ending with a WS row.

Shape shoulder

Cast off 3 (4:4:5:5) sts at beg of the next row. Work 1 row. Cast off rem 4 (5:5:6:6) sts. With RS facing, slip the centre st onto a safety pin (this marks the st), rejoin yarn and knit to end. Complete this side to match first side, reversing shapings.

NECKBAND

Join left shoulder. With RS facing, 4 mm needles and A, knit up 3 sts from right back neck, knit across 17 (17:19:19:21) sts from back neck st holder, dec 1 st in centre of these sts, knit up 3 sts from left back neck, 35 (37:39:41:43) sts down left front neck, knit marked st, knit up 35 (37:39:41:43) sts up right front neck. [93 (97:103:107:113) sts.]

Next row: Beg with a 2nd rib row, rib to within 2 sts of marked st, p2tog, p1, p2tog-tbl, rib rem 55 (57:61:63:67) sts.

Next row: Rib to within 2 sts of marked st, k2tog-tbl, k1b, k2tog, rib to end. Rib 3 more rows, dec either side of marked st as set. [83 (87:93:97:103) sts.] Cast off ribwise, dec as before.

ARMBANDS (MAKE 2)

Join right shoulder and neckband. With RS facing, 4 mm needles and A, knit up 81 (85:89:93:97) sts evenly along one armhole edge. Beg with a 2nd rib row, rib 5 rows. Cast off ribwise.

TO MAKE UP

Join side seams.

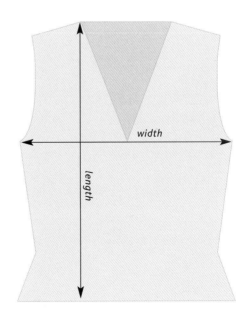

width

length

This luxurious kid mohair cardigan is gorgeously cosy and can be teamed with anything. It is worked in simple stocking stitch and has pretty heart-shaped buttons.

SILKY MOHAIR CARDIGAN

★ ☆ ☆ VERY EASY

 *Another easy-to-knit garment created in stocking stitch and with very simple shaping.*

 *ake care when working with mohair as the yarn tends to shed.*

MEASUREMENTS
To fit bust
81	86	91	97	102	cm
32	34	36	38	40	in

Actual width
86	91	96	101	106	cm
34	36	37¾	39¾	41¼	in

Actual length
45	46	47	48	49	cm
17¾	18	18½	19	19¼	in

Actual sleeve seam
43	43	46	46	46	cm
17	17	18	18	18	in

In the instructions figures are given for the smallest size first; larger sizes follow in brackets. Where only one set of figures is given this applies to all sizes.

MATERIALS
- 8 (9:10:11:12) × 25 g balls of Rowan Kidsilk Haze in 581
- Pair each of 3 mm and 3¾ mm needles
- Stitch holder
- 7 small buttons

TENSION
23 sts and 32 rows to 10 cm (4 in) measured over stocking stitch using 3¾ mm needles and yarn used double.

ABBREVIATIONS
See page 10.

CARDIGAN

BACK
With 3 mm needles and yarn used double throughout, cast on 99 (105:111:117:123) sts.
Row 1: RS. *K1, p1; rep from * to last st, k1.
Row 2: *P1, k1; rep from * to last st, p1.
Rep these 2 rows 3 times more.
Change to 3¾ mm needles. Cont in st st beg with a knit row until work measures 26 (27:27:27:27) cm (10¼ (10¾:10¾:10¾:10¾) in) from beg, ending with a WS row.

Shape armholes
Cast off 6 (6:7:7:9) sts at beg of the next 2 rows [87 (93:97:103:105) sts], then dec 1 st at each end of the next 4 rows [79 (85:89:95:97) sts], then on the 2 (2:2:4:4) foll alt rows. [75 (81:85:87:89) sts.]
Cont straight until armhole measures 19 (19:20:21:22) cm (7½ (7½:8:8¼:8¾) in) from beg of shaping, ending with a WS row.

Shape shoulders and back neck
Cast off 7 (8:8:8:9) sts at beg of the next 2 rows. [61 (65:69:71:71) sts.] Cast off 7 (8:9:9:9) sts at beg of the next row, knit until there are 11 (12:13:13:13) sts on RH needle, turn and leave rem sts on a st holder. Work on

HELPFUL HINT

To prevent mohair fibres from shedding, store balls of mohair yarn safely wrapped in polythene in the fridge.

these sts for first side. Cast off 4 sts at beg of the next row. Cast off rem 7 (8:9:9:9) sts. With RS facing, rejoin yarn and leave centre 25 (25:25:27:27) sts on a st holder. Complete this side to match first side, reversing shapings.

LEFT FRONT

With 3 mm needles and yarn used double throughout, cast on 49 (51:55:57:61) sts and work 8 rows in rib as given for Back welt, inc 0 (1:0:1:0) st in centre of last row. [49 (52:55:58:61) sts.] Change to 3¾ mm needles. Cont in st st beg with a knit row, until work measures same as Back to beg of armhole shaping, ending with a WS row.

Shape armhole

Cast off 6 (6:7:7:9) sts at beg of the next row. [43 (46:48:51:52) sts.] Work 1 row then dec 1 st at armhole edge on the next 4 rows [39 (42:44:47:48) sts], then on the 2 (2:2:4:4) foll alt rows. [37 (40:42:43:44) sts.] Cont straight until Front measures 23 (23:23:23:25) rows shorter than Back to beg of shoulder shaping, ending with a RS row.

Shape front neck

Cast off 6 (6:6:7:7) sts at beg of the next row, then dec 1 st at same edge on the next 3 rows

[28 (31:33:33:34) sts], then on the 7 foll alt rows. [21 (24:26:26:27) sts.] Work 5 (5:5:5:7) rows, ending at side edge.

Shape shoulder

Cast off 7 (8:8:8:9) sts at beg of the next row, 7 (8:9:9:9) sts on the foll alt row. Work 1 row. Cast off rem 7 (8:9:9:9) sts.

RIGHT FRONT

Work as given for Left Front, reversing shapings.

SLEEVES (MAKE 2)

With 3 mm needles and yarn used double throughout, cast on 47 (47:51:51:53) sts and work 8 rows in rib as given for Back welt. Change to 3¾ mm needles. Cont in st st beg with a knit row, at the same time inc 1 st at each end of the 5th and 2 (7:7:7:15) foll 6th rows [53 (63:67:67:85) sts], then on the 13 (10:10:10:4) foll 8th rows. [79 (83:87:87:93) sts.] Cont straight until sleeve measures 43 (43:46:46:46) cm (17 (17:18:18:18) in) from beg, ending with a WS row.

Shape sleeve top

Cast off 6 (6:7:7:8) sts at beg of the next 2 rows [67 (71:73:73:77) sts], then dec 1 st at each end of the next 12 rows [43 (47:49:49:53) sts], then on the 3 (3:4:4:4)

foll 4th rows [37 (41:41:41:45) sts], then on
the 3 (3:3:3:4) foll alt rows
[31 (35:35:35:37) sts], then on the next
6 rows. [19 (23:23:23:25) sts.]
Cast off.

NECKBAND

Join shoulders.

With RS facing and 3 mm needles and yarn
used double, knit up 30 (30:31:33:34) sts
along right front neck, 3 sts from right back
neck, knit across 25 (25:25:27:27) sts from
back neck st holder, knit up 3 sts from left
back neck, and 30 (30:31:33:34) sts along left
front neck.
[91 (91:93:99:101) sts.]
Beg with a 2nd rib row and work 7 rows in rib.
Cast off ribwise.

BUTTON BAND

With 3 mm needles and yarn used double,
cast on 7 sts. Cont in rib as given for Back
welt until band fits up left front to top of
neckband. Cast off ribwise.
Sew in place then mark the positions of
7 buttons, the first to come 1 cm (½ in) up
from cast-on edge the last 1 cm (½ in) down
from cast-off edge and the remainder spaced
evenly between.

BUTTONHOLE BAND

Work as given for Button Band making
buttonholes to correspond with markers on
left front as follows:
Buttonhole row 1: RS. Rib 3, (yo) twice,
k2tog, rib 2.
Buttonhole row 2: Rib, dropping one yo from
previous row.

TO MAKE UP

Sew sleeve tops into armholes then join side
and sleeve seams. Sew on buttons.

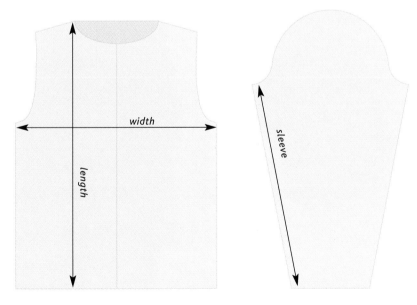

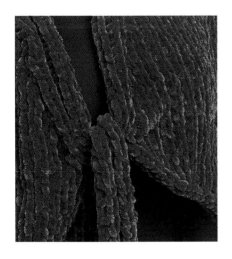  

GLAMOROUS

Τhis chapter is full of lovely items for evenings out, and you don't have to be an expert to create them. They're really versatile to wear – you can relax in style or dress up for an evening out. Sling on the cape teamed with the headband, or the bolero for added warmth, to keep the night time chill at bay, both worked in a luxurious chenille yarn. Or try the textured wrapover cardigan with frilled cuffs. Shimmer and look extra special in the fitted sweater with lace collar and cuffs, worked in a lurex yarn.

Feel special wearing this simple stocking stitch cape which ties at the front.

CAPE AND HEADBAND

★☆☆ VERY EASY

Using large size needles and a thicker yarn means that this garment is really quick and easy to knit up.

HELPFUL HINTS

- Always knit chenille yarns by taking the yarn from the 'outside' of the ball.
- To join in a new ball of chenille yarn remove approximately 5 cm (2 in) of chenille from the end of the old and beginning of the new balls by drawing fibres between your thumb-nail and index finger, leaving 5 cm (2 in) of core yarn exposed. Knot these core ends firmly together as close to the remaining chenille as possible and trim the ends.
- When sewing up garments knitted in chenille, use a plain yarn in a matching colour.

MEASUREMENTS
To fit bust

81	86	91	97	102	107	cm
32	34	36	38	40	42	in

Actual width

130	137	142	150	155	162	cm
51¼	54	56	59	61	63¾	in

Actual length

35.5	35.5	35.5	38	38	38	cm
14	14	14	15	15	15	in

In the instructions figures are given for the smallest size first; larger sizes follow in brackets. Where only one set of figures is given this applies to all sizes.

MATERIALS

- 5 (5:6:6:7:7) × 100 g balls of Sirdar Wow! in Imperial Purple 760
- Pair each of 8 mm and 7 mm needles

TENSION

8 sts and 15 rows to 10 cm (4 in) measured over stocking stitch using 7 mm needles.

ABBREVIATIONS

See page 10.

CAPE

BACK

With 8 mm needles cast on 52 (55:57:60:62:65) sts.
Change to 7 mm needles. Cont in st st beg with a knit row.
Work 6 rows, then dec 1 st at each end of the next and 2 foll 10th rows.
[46 (49:51:54:56:59) sts.]
Dec 1 st on the 1 (1:1:2:2:2) foll 4th rows [44 (47:49:50:52:55) sts], then on the 8 foll alt rows [28 (31:33:34:36:39) sts], then on the next row.
[26 (29:31:32:34:37) sts.]

Shape shoulders and back neck

Next row: K2tog, knit until there are 8 (9:10:10:11:12) sts on RH needle, turn and leave rem sts on a st holder. Dec 1 st at each end of the next 2 rows. [4 (5:6:6:7:8) sts.] Cast off.

With RS facing, rejoin yarn to rem sts, cast off 8 (9:9:10:10:11) sts and knit to last 2 sts, k2tog. Complete this side to match first side, reversing shapings.

LEFT FRONT

With 8 mm needles cast on 14 (15:16:17:18:19) sts.

Change to 7 mm needles. Cont in st st beg with a knit row.

Row 1: Knit.

Row 2: Cast on 2 sts, purl these 2 sts then purl to end.

Work 4 rows inc 1 st at front edge on every row. [20 (21:22:23:24:25) sts.]

Row 7: Dec 1 st at side edge, inc 1 st at front edge.

Work 2 rows inc 1 st at front edge on every row. [22 (23:24:25:26:27) sts.]

Work 1 row.

Inc 1 st at front edge on the next row. [23 (24:25:26:27:28) sts.]

Work 5 rows straight, place a marker at front edge on last row.

Dec 1 st at side edge on next row.

Work 1 row.

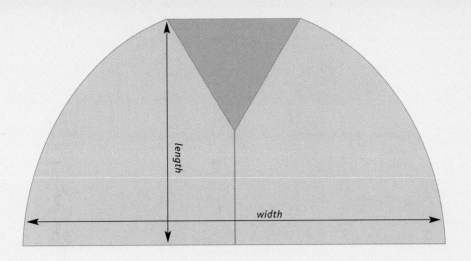

(Dec 1 st at front edge on the next row, work 3 rows straight) twice.
[20 (21:22:23:24:25) sts.]
Dec 1 st at each end of the next and 1 (1:1:3:3:3) foll 4th rows.
[16 (17:18:15:16:17) sts.]

1st, 2nd and 3rd sizes only
Work 1 row.
Dec 1 st at side edge on the next row.
Work 1 row.
Dec 1 st at each end of the next row.
[13 (14:15) sts.]

All sizes
Keeping front edge straight, cont to dec 1 st at side edge on the 6 foll alt rows
[7 (8:9:9:10:11) sts.], then on the next 3 rows.
[4 (5:6:6:7:8) sts.]
Work 1 row. Cast off.

RIGHT FRONT
Work as given for Left Front, reversing shapings.

FRONT BAND AND TIES (WORKED IN ONE PIECE)
Join side edges.
With 7 mm needles cast on 5 sts.
Row 1: RS. K2 * P1, k1; rep from * to last st, k1.
Row 2: K1 * p1, k1; rep from * to end.
Cont in rib until piece measures 34 cm (13½ in), place a marker, then cont in rib until piece fits from marker on right front to marker on left front, work a further 34 cm (13½ in). Cast off.

TO MAKE UP
Sew side seams.
Attach ties to front edge between markers.

LOWER EDGE
With RS facing and 7 mm needles, pick up and knit 34 (35:36:37:38:39) sts from tie round left front curve to side seam, 49 (52:54:57:59:62) sts along back, 34 (35:36:37:38:39) sts round right front curve to tie. [117 (122:126:131:135:140) sts.]
Knit 1 row. Change to 8 mm needles and cast off loosely.

BOBBLE AND CORD (MAKE 4)
With 7 mm needles cast on 3 sts, inc in 1st st, k1, inc in last st, 5 sts, turn and purl, turn and k1, sl 1, k2tog, psso, k1, turn, p3tog. With rem st work a cord. Knit 4 rows. Fasten off.
Attach two bobble and cords to each end of front ties.

HEADBAND
With 7 mm needles cast on 7 sts and work in rib as given for Front Band until piece reaches the desired length to fit around head. Cast off ribwise. Join seam.

Worked in a sparkly lurex yarn, this slim-fitting sweater would look good at any special occasion teamed with trousers or skirt. It is knitted in stocking stitch with a lace garter stitch border, which is made separately and sewn on afterwards.

SWEATER WITH LACE COLLAR AND CUFFS

★ ★ ★ ★ **EASY**

The lace pattern on the collar and cuffs requires some knitting skill.

Allow a little more time to complete this project as metallic yarn does take longer to work with.

HELPFUL HINTS
- Sew the collar to the neck edge using a firm back stitch to avoid the neckline stretching too much.

MEASUREMENTS
To fit bust

81	91	97	102	107	cm
32	34	36	38	40	in

Actual width

75	81	85	91	96	cm
29½	32	33½	36	37¾	in

Actual length

46	47	48	48	49	cm
18	18½	19	19	19¼	in

Actual sleeve seam (with cuff lace edging)

46	49	49	49	49	cm
18	19¼	19¼	19¼	19¼	in

In the instructions figures are given for the smallest size first; larger sizes follow in brackets. Where only one set of figures is given this applies to all sizes.

MATERIALS
- 14 (15:16:17:18) × 25 g balls of Rowan Lurex in Antique White Gold
- Pair each of 2¾ mm, 3¼ mm and 4 mm needles
- Stitch holder

TENSION
29 sts and 41 rows to 10 cm (4 in) measured over stocking stitch using 3¼ mm needles.

ABBREVIATIONS
See page 10.

SWEATER

BACK AND FRONT (ALIKE)
With 2¾ mm needles cast on 110 (118:124:132:140) sts and knit 10 rows. Change to 3¼ mm needles. Cont in st st beg with a knit row, shaping sides by dec 1 st at each end of the 5th and 5 foll 6th rows [98 (106:112:120:128) sts], then inc 1 st at each end of the 6 foll 12th rows. [110 (118:124:132:140) sts.] Cont straight until work measures 34 cm (13½ in) from beg, ending with a WS row.

Shape raglans
Cast off 6 (6:7:7:8) sts at beg of the next 2 rows [98 (106:110:118:124) sts], then dec 1 st at each end of the next and 0 (2:4:8:12) foll alt rows [96 (100:100:100:98) sts], then on the 10 (10:10:8:7) foll 4th rows. [76 (80:80:84:84) sts.] Work 1 row, ending with a WS row.

Shape front neck

Knit 10, turn and leave rem 66 (70:70:74:74) sts on a st holder. Work on these sts for first side. Cast off 4 sts at neck edge on next row. Dec 1 st at each end of the next row, then 1 st at neck edge on the next 3 rows. Fasten off last st.

With RS facing, rejoin yarn to centre sts. Cast off 56 (60:60:64:64) sts and knit to end. [10 sts.] Complete this side to match first side, reversing shapings.

SLEEVES (MAKE 2)

With 3¼ mm needles cast on 58 (58:64:64:66) sts. Cont in st st beg with a knit row, shaping sides by inc 1 st at each end of the 3rd and 2 (7:7:7:13) foll 4th rows, then on the 17 (15:15:15:11) foll 6th rows. [98 (104:110:110:116) sts.] Cont straight until Sleeve measures 33 (36:36:36:36) cm (13 (14:14:14:14) in) from beg, ending with a WS row.

Shape raglan

Cast off 6 (6:7:7:8) sts at beg of the next 2 rows. [86 (92:96:96:100) sts.] Dec 1 st at each end of the next and 20 (24:26:26:28) foll alt rows [44 (42:42:42:42) sts], then on the 1 (0:0:0:0) foll 4th row. [42 sts.] Work 3 rows. Cast off.

TO MAKE UP

Join 3 raglans leaving right back seam open.

Neckband

With RS facing and 2¾ mm needles, knit up 56 (60:60:64:64) sts from back, 37 sts from top of left sleeve, 56 (60:60:64:64) sts from front, 37 sts from top of right sleeve. [186 (194:194:202:202) sts.]
Knit 9 rows. Cast off. Join remaining raglan and neckband.
Join side and sleeve seams.

LACE FRILL NECKBAND

With 4 mm needles, cast on 25 sts and knit 1 row.
Row 1: Sl 1, k6, (yo, k2tog) 8 times, yo, k2.
Rows 2, 4, 6, 8 and 10: Knit.
Row 3: Sl 1, k9, (yo, k2tog) 7 times, yo, k2.
Row 5: Sl 1, k12, (yo, k2tog) 6 times, yo, k2.
Row 7: Sl 1, k15, (yo, k2tog) 5 times, yo, k2.
Row 9: Sl 1, k18, (yo, k2tog) 4 times, yo, k2.
Row 11: Sl 1, k29.
Row 12: Cast off 5 sts, k to end. [25 sts.]
These 12 rows form the lace edge patt.
Cont in patt until piece fits around neck edge.
Do not stretch the fabric when measuring.
Cast off.
Join cast-on and cast-off edges, then with RS of frill to WS body and seam to right back raglan seam, sew around neck edge firmly using a back stitch.

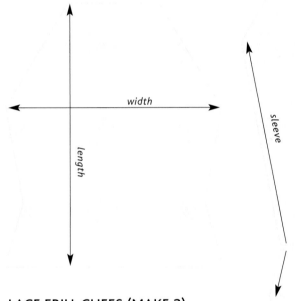

LACE FRILL CUFFS (MAKE 2)

With 4 mm needles, cast on 25 sts and knit 1 row.
Work the 12 rows of patt as given for neckband until piece fits around cuff edge.
Cast off. Join cast-on and cast-off edge, then with seam to sleeve seam, sew around cuffs edge firmly using a back stitch.

This gorgeous bolero jacket looks fabulous over a simple black dress and is great for keeping your shoulders warm on an evening out. Using large needles and a luxurious velvety chenille yarn, it is made using simple stocking stitch.

BOLERO JACKET

 *This is another simple design but requires some skill when picking up stitches around the front curves for the edges.*

 *When casting off round front edges, use a large size needle as this yarn does not stretch.*

HELPFUL HINTS
- When joining in a new ball of chenille yarn, remove approximately 5 cm (2 in) of chenille from the end of the old and beginning of the new balls by drawing the fibres between your thumbnail and index finger, leaving 5 cm (2 in) of core yarn exposed. Knot these core ends firmly together as close to the remaining chenille as possible and trim ends.
- When sewing up garments knitted in chenille yarn, use a plain yarn in a matching colour.

MEASUREMENTS
To fit bust

76–81	86–91	97–102	cm
30–32	34–36	38–40	in

Actual width

83	93	103	cm
32¾	36½	40½	in

Actual length

32	33.5	35	cm
12½	13	13¾	in

Actual sleeve seam

46 cm	
18 in	

In the instructions figures are given for the smallest size first; larger sizes follow in brackets. Where only one set of figures is given this applies to all sizes.

MATERIALS
- 5 (6:7) × 100 g balls of Sirdar Wow! in Raspberry Crush 758
- Pair of 7 mm needles
- 7 mm circular needle
- Stitch holder

TENSION
8 sts and 15 rows to 10 cm (4 in) measured over stocking stitch using 7 mm needles.

ABBREVIATIONS
See page 10.

JACKET

BACK
With 7 mm needles, cast on 33 (37:41) sts. Work 20 rows in st st beg with a knit row, ending with a WS row.

Shape armholes
Cast off 3 sts at beg of the next 2 rows. [27 (31:35) sts.] Dec 1 st at both ends of the next 3 rows [21 (25:29) sts], then cont straight until armhole measures 19 (20.5:22) cm (7½ (8¼:8¾) in) from beg of shaping, ending with a WS row.

Shape shoulders

Cast off 4 (5:6) sts at beg of next 2 rows. Leave rem 13 (15:17) sts on a st holder for back neck.

LEFT FRONT

With 7 mm needles, cast on 8 (10:12) sts. Cont in st st beg with a knit row. Work 1 row, ending at front edge.

Shape front edge

Inc 1 st at the front edge on the next 8 rows [16 (18:20) sts], then on the foll alt row [17 (19:21) sts], place a marker at the front edge on the last row. Work 9 rows straight, ending with a WS row.

Shape armhole

Cast off 3 sts at beg of next row. [14 (16:18) sts.] Work 1 row, then dec 1 st at armhole edge on the next 3 rows. [11 (13:15) sts.] Work straight until armhole measures 15 rows shorter than Back to the shoulder, ending at the front edge.

Shape front neck

Cast off 2 (3:4) sts at beg of the next row [9 (10:11) sts], then dec 1 st at neck edge on the 5 foll alt rows. [4 (5:6) sts.] Cont straight until Front measures the same as Back to the shoulder, ending with a WS row. Cast off 4 (5:6) sts.

With 7 mm needles, cast on 2 sts, * pass the first st made over the second. Cast on 1 st; rep from * until ties measure approximately 25 cm (10 in), or required length. Fasten off and attach to beg of neck shaping.

RIGHT FRONT

Work as given for Left Front, reversing shapings.

SLEEVES (MAKE 2)

With 7 mm needles cast on 18 (20:22) sts and purl 2 rows. Cont in st st beg with a knit row, inc 1 st at both ends of the 4 foll 15th rows. [26 (28:30) sts.] Cont straight until sleeve measures 46 cm (18 in) from beg, ending with a WS row.

Shape sleeve top

Cast off 3 sts at beg of the next 2 rows. [20 (22:24) sts.] Dec 1 st at both ends of the 3 foll 4th rows [14 (16:18) sts], then on the 2 (3:4) foll alt rows [10 sts], then on the next 3 rows. Cast off rem 4 sts.

TO MAKE UP

Press as instructions given on ball band. Join shoulders. Sew sleeve tops into armholes, then join side and sleeve seams.

FRONT AND LOWER EDGES

With RS facing and 7 mm long circular needle, beg at right side seam. Knit up 19 (21:23) sts to marker on Right Front, 20 sts to beg of neck shaping, 19 sts to shoulder, knit across 13 (15:17) sts from back neck st holder, knit up 19 sts down Left Front neck edge, 20 sts to marker on Left Front, 19 (21:23) sts to side seam, 33 (37:41) sts along back edge. [162 (172:182) sts.]
Cast off loosely. Join ends. Make and attach two ties (see above).

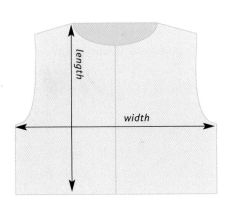

Feel extra special in this lovely cardigan worked in stocking stitch with an unusual ribbon yarn. A frilled edge on the front and cuffs, worked in a 4-ply cotton yarn adds extra femininity. It is tied round the waist to create a perfect fit.

WRAPOVER CARDIGAN

★★☆ EASY

The shaping at the front of the garment and the frilled edges require some knitting skill.

HELPFUL HINTS
- Use a firm back stitch when sewing the frill to the front edges to keep the garment in the correct shape as the main yarn is stretchy.

MEASUREMENTS
To fit bust

81	86	91	97	102	cm
32	34	36	38	40	in

Actual width

83	87	93	99	103	cm
32½	34¼	36½	39	40½	in

Actual length

48	49	50	51	52	cm
19	19¼	19½	20	20½	in

Actual sleeve seam (excluding frill)

43	43	44	44	44	cm
17	17	17½	17½	17½	in

In the instructions figures are given for the smallest size first; larger sizes follow in brackets. Where only one set of figures is given this applies to all sizes.

MATERIALS
- 9 (10:11:12:13) × 50 g balls of Rowan Cotton Braid in Renoir 353 (A)
- 2 (2:3:3:4) × 50 g balls of Rowan 4-ply Cotton in Zest 134 (B)
- Pair of 8 mm needles
- 3¼ mm long circular needle

TENSION
10½ sts and 17 rows to 10 cm (4 in) measured over stocking stitch using 8 mm needles.

ABBREVIATIONS
See page 10.

CARDIGAN

BACK
With 8 mm needles and A, cast on 38 (40:43:46:48) sts. Cont in st st beg with a knit row, at the same time, inc 1 st at both ends of the 9th and 2 foll 10th rows. [44 (46:49:52:54) sts.] Work a further 11 (13:13:15:15) rows straight, ending with a WS row.

Shape armholes
Cast off 3 (3:4:4:4) sts at beg of the next 2 rows [38 (40:41:44:46) sts], then dec 1 st at both ends of the next 4 rows. [30 (32:33:36:38) sts.] Work a further 28 (28:30:30:32) rows, ending with a WS row.

Shape shoulders
Cast off 4 sts at beg of the next 2 rows, then 3 (3:3:4:4) sts at beg of the next 2 rows. Cast off rem 16 (18:19:20:22) sts.

LEFT FRONT

With 8 mm needles and A, cast on 34 (35:36: 38:39) sts. Cont in st st, beg with a knit row.

Shape front edge

Work 40 (42:42:44:44) rows as follows: work 2 rows. Dec 1 st at front edge on the next and 2 foll alt rows. Work 1 row.

Next row: Inc 1 st at side edge and dec 1 at front edge. [31 (32:33:35:36) sts.] Dec 1 st at front edge on the 4 foll alt rows. Work 1 row.

Next row: Inc 1 st at side edge and dec 1 st at front edge. [27 (28:29:31:32) sts.]

Dec 1 st at front edge on the 3 (4:4:4:4) foll alt rows. Work 3 (1:1:1:1) rows.

Next row: Inc 1 st at side edge and dec 1 (0:0:1:1) st at front edge. Work 3 (1:1:3:3) rows. [24 (25:26:27:28) sts.]

Dec 1 st at front edge on the next and 1 (2:2:2:2) foll 4th rows.
[22 (22:23:24:25) sts.]
Work 3 rows, ending at side edge.

Shape armhole

Cast off 3 (3:4:4:4) sts at beg of the next row and dec 1 st at end of row.
[18 (18:18:19:20) sts.] Work 1 row.
Dec 1 st at armhole edge on the next 2 rows, then dec 1 st at both ends of the next row, then 1 st at armhole edge on the next row. Keeping armhole edge straight, work 2 rows, then dec 1 st at front edge on the next and

5 (5:5:5:6) foll 4th rows until 7 (7:7:8:8) sts remain. Work straight until Front measures same as Back to beg of shoulder shaping, ending at side edge.

Shape shoulder

Cast off 4 sts at beg of the next row. Work 1 row then cast off rem 3 (3:3:4:4) sts.

RIGHT FRONT

With 8 mm needles and A, cast on 34 (35:36:38:39) sts. Cont in st st, beg with a purl row. Cont as given for Left Front, reversing shapings.

SLEEVES (MAKE 2)

With 8 mm needles and A, cast on 22 (22:24:26:28) sts. Cont in st st beg with a knit row, at the same time, inc 1 st at both ends of the 7th and 6 foll 8th rows. [36 (36: 38:40:42) sts.] Cont straight until sleeve measures 43 (43:44:44:44) cm (17 (17:17½: 17½:17½) in) from beg, ending with a WS row.

Shape sleeve top

Cast off 3 (3:4:4:4) sts at beg of the next 2 rows. [30 (30:30:32:34) sts.] Dec 1 st at both ends of the next 2 rows [26 (26:26:28: 30) sts], then on the 2 foll 4th rows [22 (22: 22:24:26) sts], then on the 2 (2:2:3:4) foll alt rows [18 sts], then on the next 4 rows.
Cast off rem 10 sts.

CUFFS (MAKE 2)

With 3¼ mm circular needle and B, cast on 121 (131:131:141:141) sts and purl 2 rows. Cont in st st beg with a knit row and work 9 rows.

Dec row 1: P1, (p2tog) to end. [61 (66:66:71:71) sts.] Work 3 rows.

Dec row 2: WS (K1, k2tog) to last 1 (0:0:2:2) sts, k1 (0:0:2:2). [41 (44:44:48:48) sts.] Knit 6 rows. Cast off.

FRONT FRILL

With 3¼ mm circular needles and B, cast on 601 (651:651:701:701) sts and purl 2 rows. Cont in st st beg with a knit row and work 9 rows.

Dec row 1: P1, (p2tog) to end. [301 (326:326:351:351) sts.] Work 3 rows, ending with a RS row. Cast on 41 (44:44:48:48) sts for under band. [342 (370:370:399:399) sts.]

Dec row 2: WS. Knit 41 (44:44:48:48) sts, (k1, k2tog) to last 1 (2:2:0:0) sts, k1 (2:2:0:0). [242 (262:262:282:282) sts.] Knit 8 rows. Cast off.

LOWER BAND

Join shoulders. Sew sleeve tops into armholes, then join side and sleeve seams. With 8 mm circular needle and A, cast on 7 sts.

Row 1: Sl 1, k1, (p1, k1) twice, k1b.

Row 2: Sl 1, p1, (k1, p1) twice, k1b.

Rep these 2 rows to end until Band measures 30 cm (12 in) for the tie on the right front, place a marker, then cont until band will fit from shaped edge on right front around cast-on edge on right front, back and left front with approximately 90 cm (35 in) extra for tie. With marker at right front slope, sew in position as you go along, adjusting length to allow the band to wrap around the body and tie at the front.

TO MAKE UP

Join short ends of cuff frills. With RS of frill to RS of sleeve edge, position seams tog and stitch tog. With RS of frill to WS of main body, sew frill in position, reverse seam on under band. Fold frill over to RS of main body and topstitch down along the first row, worked in g st to secure.

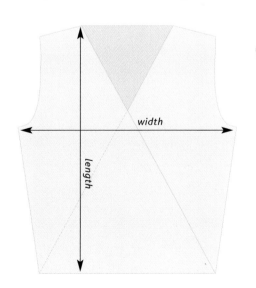

YARN INFORMATION

Rowan 4 Ply Cotton: 100% cotton. 170 m/182 yd per 50 g (1¾ oz) ball.

Rowan Biggy Print: 100% merino wool. 30 m/33 yd per 100 g (3½ oz) ball.

Rowan Big Wool: 100% merino wool. 80 m/87 yd per 100 g (3½ oz) ball.

Rowan Big Wool Tuft: 97% merino wool, 3% nylon. 25 m/27 yd per 50 g (1¾ oz) ball.

Rowan Chunky Cotton Chenille: 100% cotton. 140 m/153 yd per 100 g (3½ oz) ball.

Rowan Chunky Print: 100% wool. 100 m/110 yd per 100 g (3½ oz) ball.

Rowan Cork: 95% merino wool, 5% nylon. 110 m/120 yd per 50 g (1 3/4 oz) ball.

Rowan Cotton Braid: 68% cotton, 22% viscose, 10% linen. 50 m/55 yd per 50 g (1¾ oz) ball.

Rowan Cotton Glace: 100% cotton. 115 m/126 yd per 50 g (1¾ oz) ball.

Rowan Handknit DK Cotton: 100% cotton. 85 m/90 yd per 50 g (1¾ oz) ball.

Rowan Kidsilk Haze: 70% super kid mohair, 30% silk. 210 m/229 yd per 25 g (1 oz) ball.

Rowan Lurex Shimmer: 80% viscose, 20% polyester. 95 m/103 yd per 25 g (1 oz) ball.

Rowan Plaid: 42% merino wool, 30 % acrylic fibre, 28% superfine alpaca. 100 m/110 yd per 100 g (3½ oz) ball.

Rowan Polar: 60% pure new wool, 30% alpaca, 10% acrylic. 100 m/110 yd per 100 g (3½ oz) ball.

Rowan Ribbon Twist: 70% wool, 25% acrylic, 5% polyamide. 60 m/66 yd per 100 g (3½ oz) ball.

Rowan Summer Tweed: 79% silk, 30% cotton. 108 m/118 yd per 50 g (1¾ oz) ball.

Rowan Wool Cotton: 50% merino wool, 50% cotton. 113 m/124 yd per 50 g (1¾ oz) ball.

Rowan Yorkshire Tweed Aran: 100% pure new wool. 160 m/175 yd per 100 g (3½ oz) ball.

Rowan Yorkshire Tweed Chunky: 100% pure new wool. 100 m/110 yd per 100 g (3½ oz) ball.

Sirdar Bigga: 50% wool, 50% acrylic. 40 m/44 yd per 100 g (3½ oz) ball.

Sirdar Denim Chunky: 60% acrylic, 25% cotton, 15% wool. 156 m/170 yd per 100 g (3½ oz) ball.

Sirdar New Fizz: 72% nylon, 19% acrylic, 9% polyester. 75 m/82 yd per 50 g (1¾ oz) ball.

Sirdar Wow: 100% polyester. 58 m/63 yd per 100 g (3½ oz) ball.

Sirdar Yo-Yo: 74% acrylic, 14% wool, 12% polyester. 800 m/874 yd per 400 g (14 oz) ball.

SUPPLIERS AND USEFUL ADDRESSES

UK

Rowan Yarns
Green Lane Mill
Holmfirth
West Yorkshire
HD9 2DX
Tel: (01484) 681881
Fax: (01484) 687920
Email: mail@knitrowan.com
www.knitrowan.com
Call for details of your nearest
stockist or order online

Sirdar Spinning Ltd
Flanshaw Lane
Alverthorpe
Wakefield
West Yorkshire
WF2 9ND
Tel: (01924) 371501
Fax: (01924) 290506
Email: orders@sirdar.co.uk
www.sirdar.co.uk
Call for details of your nearest
stockist or order online

USA

Knitting Fever Inc.
PO Box 502
Roosevelt
New York 11575
Tel: (516) 546 3600
Fax: (516) 546 6871
Email:
webmaster@knittingfever.com
Stockist of Sirdar yarns

Rowan USA
4 Townsend West
Suite 8
Nashua
New Hampshire 03064
Tel: (603) 886 5041/5043
Email wfibers@aol.com
Call for details of your nearest
stockist

AUSTRALIA

Australian Country Spinners
314 Albert Street
Brunswick
Victoria 3056
Tel: (03) 9380 3888
Stockist of Rowan yarns

Creative Images
PO Box 106
Hastings
Victoria 3915
Australia
Tel: (03) 5979 1555
Fax: (03) 5979 1544
Email:
creative@peninsula.starway.net.au
Stockist of Sirdar yarns

SOUTH AFRICA

Arthur Bales Ltd
62 4th Avenue
Linden
Johannesburg 2195
Tel: (027) 118 882 401
Fax: (027) 117 826 137
Email: Arthur@new.co.za
Stockist of Rowan yarns

Saprotex International (Pty)
PO Box 1293
East London 5200
Tel: (027) 43 763 1551
Fax: (027) 43 763 1929
Email: tbarratt@bertrand.co.za
Stockist of Sirdar yarns

INDEX

ACKNOWLEDGEMENTS

I would like to thank all those involved in the creation of this book, especially to Rosemary Wilkinson and Clare Sayer for their continued support and organisation. Thank you to Sian Irvine for her lovely photographs, models Emma, Jo, Kat, Natalie and Sarah and Isobel Gillan for her design.

Special thanks go to the pattern checker Marilyn Wilson. Also to David Rawson and Pauline Brown at Sirdar, and Linda Parkhouse and all at Rowan, who helped to sort out the yarn requirements. A huge thank you to both Sirdar and Rowan for producing such lovely yarns, which help to inspire all the garments I design. And where would I be without my loyal knitters, Margaret Craik, Helen Hawe, Thelma Seager, Irene Hall and Christine D'Acunzo? Who always amaze me by their speed and efficiency to turn garments around, even at the busiest times of the year.

I shall always be indebted to the magazines and spinners who commission my designs and who have now become special people in my life. Especially Elena Costella and Allison Stewart who work for the D C Thompson group of magazines and Margaret Maino and Beth Johnson from Creative Plus Publishing Ltd.

I have to thank my family for getting my interest in knitting going in the first place, and also for putting up with being surrounded by wool for all these years, and my artistic temperament!

A very special thank you to my daughter Sarah, who soon became proficient in the skill, and helped with the knitting in this book, and to Robert my son, because he's my son. I suppose they will always have this image of their mum with knitting needles and wool.

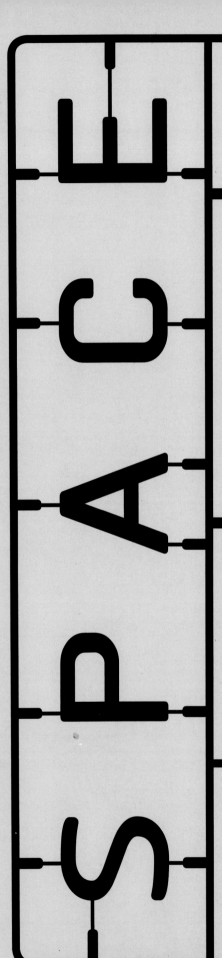

SPACE

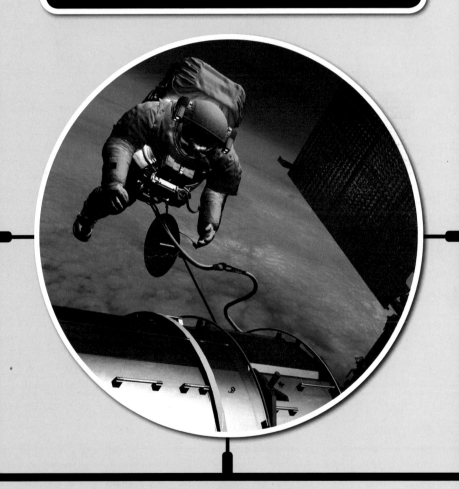

ADVENTURES IN
STEAM

Richard Spilsbury

WAYLAND
www.waylandbooks.co.uk

First published in Great Britain in 2017 by Wayland

Copyright © Hodder and Stoughton Limited, 2017

Produced for Wayland by
White-Thomson Publishing Ltd
www.wtpub.co.uk

Series editor: Izzi Howell
Designer: Rocket Design (East Anglia) Ltd
Illustrations: Rocket Design (East Anglia) Ltd
In-house editor: Julia Bird

ISBN: 978 1 5263 0479 7
10 9 8 7 6 5 4 3 2 1

Wayland
An imprint of
Hachette Children's Group
Part of Hodder & Stoughton
Carmelite House
50 Victoria Embankment
London EC4Y 0DZ

An Hachette UK Company
www.hachette.co.uk
www.hachettechildrens.co.uk

Printed in China

Picture acknowledgements:
Julian Baker: 11 and 45l; NASA: 3, 5t, 6, 12, 17t, 17b, 18t, 18c, 18b, 19t, 19c, 20, 22, 23, 24, 26, 27, 29t, 29b, 30b, 35b, 37, 39, 42, JPL-Caltech 5b, 36, 38, Pat Corkery, United Launch Alliance 10, Bigelow Aerospace 21, Dmitri Gerondidakis 31b, ESA, and the Hubble Heritage Team (STScI/AURA) 33, CXC/M.Weiss 34t, JHUAPL/SwRI 34c, JPL-Caltech/UCAL/MPS/DLR/IDA 34b, JPL-Caltech/MSSS 40, 41t, MSFC 43, MarsScientific.com and Clay Center Observatory 45; Shutterstock: iurii cover and title page, RJ Design 7, Jorg Hackemann 8, Everett Historical 9, 28, 30c, 31t, 31c, Andrey Armyagov 14, Harvepino 15, Delpixel 25, AuntSpray 30t, MarcelClemens 32, Belish 35t, solarseven 35c, ESB Professional 41b; Wikimedia: RIA Novosti archive/Alexander Mokletsov / 19b, Jeff Foust44.

All design elements from Shutterstock.

CONTENTS

BEYOND OUR PLANET

WHEN WE LOOK UP, WE SEE CLOUDS AND SKY,
BUT BEYOND EARTH'S ATMOSPHERE LIES
THE MYSTERIOUS REALM OF SPACE. FAR FROM OUR PLANET
THERE IS A WEALTH OF OTHER PLANETS, STARS AND MANY
MORE OBJECTS, FROM ASTEROIDS AND COMETS TO BLACK HOLES.

The Earth is one of eight planets circling, or orbiting, a star we call the Sun. Together they are called the solar system. The Sun is a massive ball of burning gas, hot enough to warm our planet even though it is billions of kilometres away. It is just one of a vast number of stars clustered into our galaxy. The universe is made up of billions of such galaxies and the vast gaps in between objects, which contain nothing but floating dust and gases.

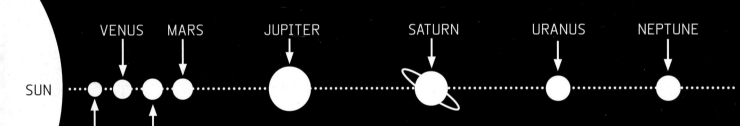

SUN

MERCURY   EARTH

VENUS   MARS

JUPITER

SATURN

URANUS

NEPTUNE

Planets in our solar system range in size from Jupiter, over 300 times bigger than Earth, to Mercury, less than half Earth's size. The four planets closest to the Sun are warm, rocky planets, but the outer planets are giant, cold, spinning balls of gas.

" MATHS TALK

An astronomical unit (AU) is the distance from Earth to the Sun, which is 150 million km. But the next nearest star is around 270,000 AU away from Earth. Scientists need larger units called light years to measure the universe. One light year is the distance light travels in one year, or 9, 461, 000, 000, 000 km. The universe is around 93 billion light years across!

People have been fascinated by and studied space for centuries using ever more advanced technology, from simple telescopes to complex sensors on spacecraft. Some lucky people have even visited and experienced space and had the chance to look down on their home planet from above.

THINKING OUTSIDE THE BOX!

In 1931, Belgian priest and scientist Georges Lemaître proposed the new idea that the universe started with one giant, incredibly hot explosion around 14 billion years ago. He called it the Big Bang. For centuries before this, people widely believed the Earth and everything in space was created by God. In the 1960s, astronomers finally found proof for the Big Bang theory. They detected radiation in the universe that could only be explained as the leftover energy from the explosion.

SCIENCE TALK

Most scientists now agree that the universe was born from a dot of matter far smaller than a pinhead. During the Big Bang, it suddenly expanded outwards. Over millions of years, stars, planets and other objects formed. Scientists know the universe is still expanding today because galaxies are getting further away from Earth and each other.

The galaxy containing our solar system is called the Milky Way because light from stars makes it glow white in the night sky. This is a nearby galaxy of a similar shape to the Milky Way.

GETTING TO SPACE

AFTER CENTURIES OF WONDERING WHAT IT WOULD BE LIKE TO GO TO SPACE, HUMANS STARTED TO MAKE TRIPS THERE FROM THE 1960S ONWARDS. THE CHALLENGES OF REACHING SPACE THEN, AS NOW, WERE ALL ABOUT OVERCOMING THE POWERFUL FORCE OF GRAVITY.

Gravity is the downwards pull towards Earth or other large objects. The pull of gravity on your body, for example, makes you fall if you jump up. Weight is a measure of the force of gravity on any mass (measure of amount of matter). To rise through the air, any aircraft needs to produce a push or thrust upwards greater than its weight to escape gravity's pull. All space missions have produced the massive thrusts needed to lift heavy spacecraft with rocket engines.

The earliest rockets were fireworks made from hollow bamboo pieces packed with gunpowder. Lighting the gunpowder created thrust by shooting hot gases downwards. But the direction of these and later missiles was inaccurate and hard to control. Fast forward to 1926, when scientist Robert Goddard tested the first modern rocket. Goddard's rocket flew for less than three seconds and rose for just under 12.5 m, but demonstrated a technology that would be developed into space rockets.

Goddard dreamed of seeing Earth from space as a child and when first developing rockets was ridiculed as 'Moon Man'. However, his vision of rocket flight helped turn space flight into reality.

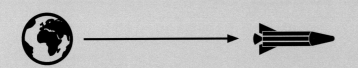

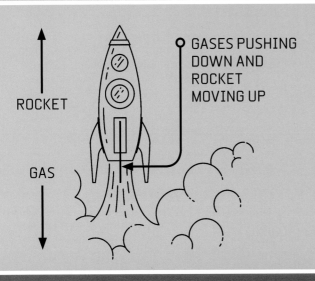

ROCKET

GAS

GASES PUSHING DOWN AND ROCKET MOVING UP

SCIENCE TALK

Forces always work in pairs. This is called action and reaction. The action of gases pushing down causes a reaction in the opposite direction and so the rocket is pushed upwards. Goddard's rocket used liquid fuels of gasoline and oxygen in a combustion chamber to achieve lift-off. These provided more controlled thrust than solid fuels of the time because a certain amount could be burnt at a time.

TECHNOLOGY TALK

Goddard improved his rocket design by adding technology. He developed a system of springs and weights that could control the angle of thrust to keep the rocket climbing vertically, a compartment onboard to store scientific instruments and even a parachute that would deploy once fuel had run out to slow the fall of the rocket back to Earth. All of these technologies have been used on space rockets and other flying machines ever since.

MATHS TALK

Solid fuels in Goddard's time gave rockets a two per cent efficiency of converting the energy in fuel into thrust. Goddard's design improvements, including using a specially shaped nozzle for gases, raised the efficiency to 63 per cent. Even today's rockets can rarely achieve more than 70 per cent.

FROM THE 1950S ONWARDS, WEAPONS OF WAR WERE

THE FIRST SPACE ROCKETS

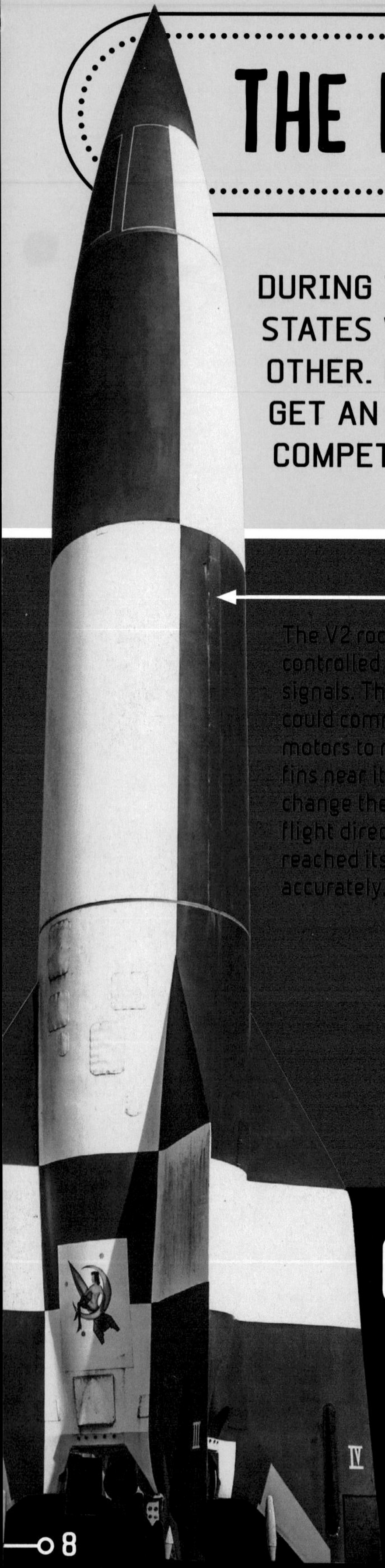

DURING THE 1950S, THE SOVIET UNION AND THE UNITED STATES WERE ENEMIES AND WANTED TO OUTDO EACH OTHER. ONE WAY TO SHOW THEIR DOMINANCE WAS TO GET AN ASTRONAUT INTO SPACE BEFORE THE OTHER. THIS COMPETITION BECAME KNOWN AS THE SPACE RACE.

The V2 rocket was controlled by radio signals. These could command motors to move the fins near its base to change the rocket's flight direction so it reached its target accurately.

The rocket had showed its power in the Second World War (1939–1945), when German forces rained down V2 rockets onto London. These liquid-fuelled rockets, launched from Germany, flew 80 km high in the air and then exploded on reaching their target in the UK. The space race happened because each side realised such powerful rockets could carry not only bombs, but also astronauts and spacecraft into space. In 1942, the first German rocket reached space.

After the war, German scientists involved with V2 development teamed up with Russian and US rocket engineers. They helped to build the first space rockets for each side and achieved many more firsts:

OCT 1957

The Soviet Union launch a new Semyorka rocket to put the first ever satellite, Sputnik 1, in space.

APRIL 1961

The Vostok-K rocket launches Soviet astronaut Yuri Gagarin to become the first man in space.

MAY 1961

The US Redstone rocket reaches space, but it is not powerful enough to get US astronaut Alan Shepard into orbit.

The liftoff of Apollo 11 on a Saturn V rocket in 1969. The Saturn V rocket was 111 m tall and capable of carrying over 48 tonnes to the Moon. It had a total of ten engines for thrusting it through Earth's atmosphere. It remains the largest space rocket ever built.

THINKING OUTSIDE THE BOX!

The first living things to reach space from Earth were fruit flies in 1947. Ten years later, a dog became the first mammal to leave our planet. Scientists used animals to find out more about the dangers of take-off, high-speed flight and time in space before humans made the trip.

ENGINEERING TALK

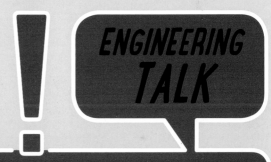

The first design for the Sputnik 1 satellite was too heavy for their existing launch vehicle to lift into space, so Russian space engineers reduced its size and weight. Rocket engineers need to carefully consider the weight of the payload (what a rocket carries, from equipment to astronauts) when deciding on the amount of engine thrust a rocket needs.

★ **FEB 1962**

The more powerful Atlas rocket takes US astronaut John Glenn into orbit.

★ **DEC 1965**

Two US astronauts spend two weeks in space.

★ **JULY 1969**

A Russian N1 rocket capable of travelling to the Moon explodes on the launch pad, causing the largest explosion in the

★ **JULY 1969**

The Saturn V launches the US Apollo 11 mission, whose astronauts complete the first Moon landing

REACHING SPACE TODAY

TODAY'S ROCKETS OR LAUNCH VEHICLES COME IN MANY SIZES, DEPENDING ON THE PAYLOAD THEY NEED TO CARRY INTO SPACE. THE LARGEST ARE CALLED HEAVY-LIFT VEHICLES, WHICH CAN CARRY OVER 50 TONNES INTO SPACE, WHEREAS SMALL-LIFT VEHICLES CAN CARRY TWO TONNES AT MOST.

Space rockets are streamlined, with a long, thin shape that helps them move faster through the atmosphere. Objects moving forward through air are pushed back by it and this friction reduces their speed. A streamlined shape reduces the surface area for air to push against. Smooth sides also reduce the friction or air resistance (drag) between air and the rocket's surface.

" MATHS TALK

Only around 1 per cent of a rocket's weight is its payload. Most of the rest is the propulsion system of engines and fuel. For example, the launch vehicle Ariane weighs nearly 800 tonnes at take-off. Of this, 550 tonnes is solid fuel in the boosters, which is used up in the first two minutes of flight, and 175 tonnes is liquid fuel in the main section or stage. That's 90 per cent of its total weight. "

A rocket needs to be tough enough to withstand massive vibrations from its engines while they fire. The inner frame is formed from vertical beams attached to hoops up the length of the vehicle. A smooth metal skin is shaped around this frame. Both are made from strong but lightweight metals such as aluminium alloys. In parts such as the tip and fuel tank the skin is covered with special carbon fibre heat shields. These reduce the heating of the skin and contents due to friction.

Many launch vehicles, such as Ariane V, have several stages or parts used for different legs of the journey to space.

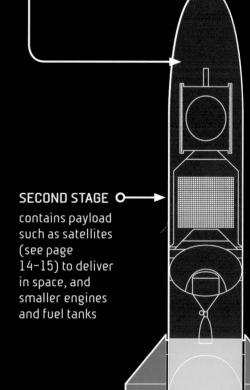

THINKING OUTSIDE THE BOX!

Engineers are designing launch vehicles that are not rockets. One idea is to use a tough balloon filled with helium to lift a small launch vehicle that fires its thrusters around 32 km above Earth. Another idea is to use a maglev train on an upcurved track to launch a type of space plane. Maglevs use the push of magnets against each other to lift trains above tracks, eliminating friction and increasing speed.

PROJECT

Design an aerodynamic rocket to carry a payload of passengers.

- ■ What source of thrust would you use?

- ■ Why might you need tail fins at the end?

- ■ How would you adapt the design to carry a heavier payload?

SECOND STAGE contains payload such as satellites (see page 14–15) to deliver in space, and smaller engines and fuel tanks

MAIN STAGE contains giant fuel tanks and thruster engines to get it to space, where it detaches and falls to Earth

BOOSTERS solid fuel rockets that give extra thrust at take-off when a rocket is at its heaviest, before detaching and falling into the ocean

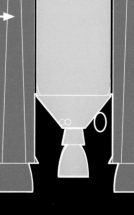

IN ORBIT

SPACE BEGINS AROUND 100 KM ABOVE THE EARTH'S SURFACE. HERE THE FORCE OF GRAVITY FROM EARTH IS WEAKER THAN ON THE PLANET'S SURFACE AND THERE IS SO LITTLE AIR THAT DRAG IS NEGLIGIBLE. SPACECRAFT CAN ORBIT EARTH USING VERY LITTLE THRUST AND FUEL.

Spacecraft control their orbits using small thrusters controlled by computers that nudge them left or right, faster or slower, to ensure they remain at the right speed and height above Earth.

Moving in orbit around Earth relies on gravity. Without it, a rocket would continue outwards on a straight path to outer space. Gravity's pull changes the craft's straight motion into a circular orbit. When you throw a ball hard, it travels straight for longer before arcing to Earth than if you throw it softly. In the same way, spacecraft need to move fast to stop gravity from dragging them back towards our planet. Spacecraft orbit at different heights from Earth to avoid flying too close to each other. Those orbiting closer to Earth need to go fastest, because gravity's pull is stronger.

SCIENCE TALK

The force of gravity is so strong that space launch vehicles must reach a speed known as escape velocity to break free of its pull. This is at least 11 km per second (40,000 kph). Once in orbit, a craft must continue to fly at around 27,000 kph to prevent it from being pulled gradually back to Earth.

Spacecraft are not the only man-made objects orbiting Earth. There are also around 370,000 pieces of space junk. These orbiting objects include parts of exploded rockets, disused satellites (see page 14–15), and tools or gloves accidentally dropped by astronauts. Space junk is hazardous because it can fly into, and even punch a hole through, a spacecraft in orbit.

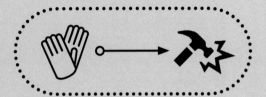

ENGINEERING TALK

Engineers are thinking of solutions to deal with space junk. CleanSpace One is a satellite that hunts down a disused satellite in orbit and uses a mechanical grabber to pick it up. Then both satellites head for Earth. Other ideas include stretching out tough fishing nets between spacecraft to trap junk and using special sensors to spot and track junk movements so that spacecraft can manoeuvre out of its way.

SATELLITES

ON A CLEAR NIGHT, YOU MIGHT SEE A DOT OF LIGHT SLOWLY CROSSING THE DARK SKY. THIS IS MOST LIKELY TO BE AN ARTIFICIAL SATELLITE ORBITING IN SPACE. THERE ARE THOUSANDS OF ARTIFICIAL, OR MAN-MADE, SATELLITES ABOVE EARTH THAT HELP US IN DIFFERENT WAYS.

Some satellites take pictures of Earth to help meteorologists predict weather patterns or allow geographers to make maps. Some take pictures of the Sun, other planets, black holes or distant galaxies to help scientists understand space. Other satellites are used to send TV signals and phone calls around the world.

SCIENCE TALK !

TV and phone signals travel in straight lines, so they can be blocked by mountains or tall buildings. Today, TV signals and phone calls are beamed up to a satellite, which instantly sends them back down to different locations on Earth.

Some satellites are battery powered but most are fuelled by solar panels. Solar panels convert the energy in sunlight into electricity. Satellites have an antenna to send and receive data, such as phone messages and navigation instructions. They have sensors that check they are facing the right way and small rocket thrusters to adjust their direction.

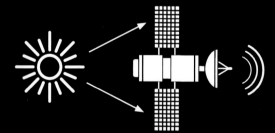

Weather satellites have cameras that take images of clouds and beam them to weather stations on Earth. Meteorologists can use images of a hurricane like this to track its movement and warn people in its path to get to safety.

GPS, or Global Positioning System, satellites help us work out exactly where we are on Earth. Each satellite transmits information about its position and the time. GPS receivers work out how far away each satellite is based on how long it takes for the signals to arrive. They use this information to pinpoint your location.

MATHS TALK

GPS receivers work by trilateration. Let's say you are on a hill with three satellites in space above. Calculating your distance from satellite 1 tells us you must be located somewhere in the red circle. If you calculate distances from satellites 2 and 3 as well, your location is where the three circles intersect.

THE MOON

THE MOON IS EARTH'S CLOSEST NEIGHBOUR. IT IS A NATURAL SATELLITE THAT TAKES ABOUT A MONTH TO ORBIT OUR PLANET. IT IS THE ONLY OBJECT IN SPACE THAT HUMANS HAVE SET FOOT ON.

The Moon probably formed about 4.5 billion years ago from debris thrown into space after a vast object crashed into Earth. Unlike Earth, the Moon has a thin, weak atmosphere that cannot protect it from the extreme heat of the Sun, or hold on to the Sun's warmth to stop it freezing at night. It is airless, waterless and lifeless.

SCIENCE TALK

The Moon is much smaller than Earth but it is still large enough to have a gravitational force that affects our planet. The oceans rise and fall up and down the coastline in tides because the Moon's gravity pulls the oceans that are directly below it.

ART TALK

During the Moon's orbit of Earth, the Sun only lights up the side of the Moon that faces towards it. Its appearance changes as the angle at which we see the Moon changes over the month. We may see a crescent, full or new Moon for example.

The first men to walk on the Moon landed there in the Apollo 11 spacecraft in 1969. They had to wear spacesuits to provide them with air and to protect them from the Sun's harmful radiation. They explored the Moon's surface for over two hours, taking film and photos and collecting 22 kg of rocks to study back on Earth.

Gravity's pull on the surface of the Moon is one-sixth of Earth's, which is why astronauts look as if they are bouncing across its surface rather than walking. Without rain, wind, or water to erode astronauts' footprints, they will probably stay there forever!

THINKING OUTSIDE THE BOX!

Astronauts on the Apollo missions left reflectors on the Moon. Scientists bounce a laser off the reflectors and measure how long it takes for the beam to reach Earth again. Using their knowledge of the speed of light, they can work out the distance between the Moon and Earth to within millimetres.

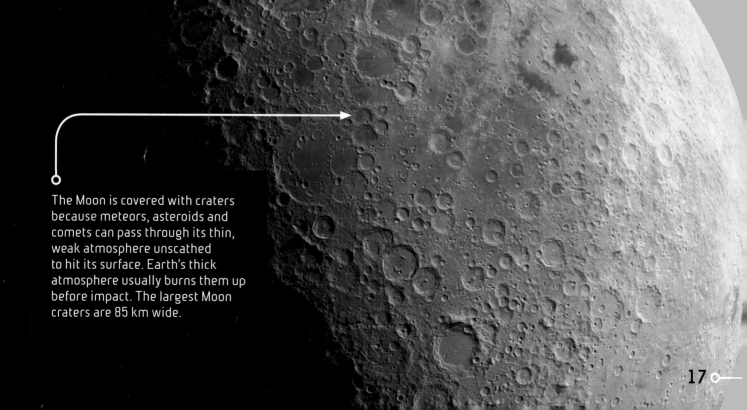

The Moon is covered with craters because meteors, asteroids and comets can pass through its thin, weak atmosphere unscathed to hit its surface. Earth's thick atmosphere usually burns them up before impact. The largest Moon craters are 85 km wide.

HALL OF FAME: ASTRONAUTS

MOST OF THE DISCOVERIES AND ACHIEVEMENTS MADE IN SPACE WOULD NOT HAVE BEEN POSSIBLE WITHOUT THE BRAVE MEN AND WOMEN WHO TOOK PART IN THE DARING AND DANGEROUS EARLY FLIGHTS INTO SPACE. THESE ASTRONAUTS TRAVELLED INTO SPACE WITHOUT KNOWING THE RISKS TO THE HUMAN BODY OR IF THEY WOULD EVER RETURN TO EARTH.

YURI GAGARIN (1934-1968)

Yuri Gagarin was a fighter pilot who became an instant worldwide celebrity when he became the first human in space on 12 April 1961. His Vostok 1 spacecraft orbited Earth at 27,400 kph and at his highest point, he found himself about 327 km above Earth. Gagarin died in a crash at the age of 34 after a routine plane flight went wrong.

JOHN GLENN (1921-2016)

John Glenn was the first US astronaut to orbit the Earth. His 1962 flight made the USA a serious contender in the space race with the Soviet Union. In 1988, aged 77, he became the oldest astronaut when he flew onboard the space shuttle *Discovery* (see page 28-29). His mission was to take part in experiments on the effects of living in space on older people.

NEIL ARMSTRONG (1930-2012)

Neil Armstrong was the mission commander on the 1969 Apollo 11 flight, during which he became the first person to walk on the Moon. He famously said, 'That's one small step for (a) man; one giant leap for mankind'. With fellow astronaut Buzz Aldrin, he spent over two hours on the Moon, studying the surface and collecting rocks.

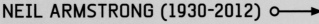

○ JAMES 'JIM' LOVELL (1928–)

Jim Lovell made four space flights and spent over 700 hours in space but he is most famous as commander of the ill-fated Apollo 13 mission in 1970, which suffered a serious explosion two days into the flight. Lovell and his crew narrowly survived the disaster and, with help from mission control, returned to Earth safely. In the 1995 movie *Apollo 13*, Lovell is played by Tom Hanks.

○ SALLY RIDE (1951–2012)

On 18 June 1983, Sally Ride became the first American woman to fly in space. She was a crew member on space shuttle *Challenger* missions, using the robotic arm she had helped develop. Back on Earth, she began NASA's EarthKAM project that lets schoolchildren take pictures of Earth using a camera on the International Space Station.

VALENTINA TERESHKOVA (1937–) ○

Valentina Tereshkova was a Russian parachutist-turned-astronaut. On 16 June 1963, she became the first woman to fly in space. During the 70.8-hour flight, her spacecraft Vostok 6 made 48 orbits of Earth. Soon after lift-off, she had to fix a problem on board after discovering that the settings for re-entry were wrong and would have sent her out into space rather than back to Earth!

THE INTERNATIONAL SPACE STATION

THE INTERNATIONAL SPACE STATION (ISS) IS THE LARGEST SPACECRAFT ORBITING EARTH. ASTRONAUTS AND SCIENTISTS FROM THE USA, RUSSIA, JAPAN AND EUROPE LIVE HERE FOR MONTHS AT A TIME, STUDYING SPACE AND ANALYSING HOW THE HUMAN BODY COPES WITH LIVING THERE.

The ISS was constructed in space from modules that were delivered piece by piece by 40 missions between 1998 and 2011. Its design was based in part on successful earlier space stations, including Skylab and Mir. The ISS is 74 m long and 110 m wide, larger than a football pitch. On a clear night, you can see the ISS from Earth as it is the third brightest object in the sky, after the Sun and Moon.

The ISS orbits the Earth 16 times a day at a height of 320 km above Earth's surface. This vast structure would collapse under its own weight if it moved into Earth's atmosphere and experienced our planet's powerful gravity.

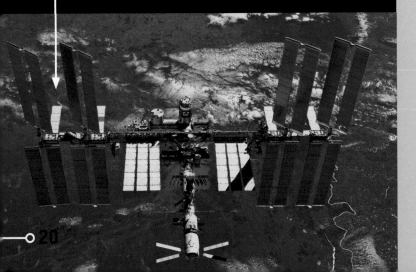

MATHS TALK

Shapes matter on the ISS. On Earth, structures like bridges use triangles and beams for strength. The framework of the ISS is made up of many such triangular structures and beams. The modules where astronauts live and work are shaped like cans and spheres. On Earth, fizzy drinks come in cans with no corners weak enough to burst under the pressure of the gassy liquid inside. In space, similar shapes can contain the pressurised atmosphere the astronauts need to breathe and survive.

The ISS has about the same amount of room as a five-bedroom house, accommodating a crew of six people, plus visitors. Reaching out from the sides of the space station are arms holding wide, flat solar panels. These are designed to capture enough of the Sun's energy to supply the ISS with ample electricity. The ISS also contains small spacecraft that astronauts can use to escape to Earth in case of an emergency!

ENGINEERING TALK

Like space rockets, the ISS is made from very strong and lightweight metals such as aluminium, titanium and high-grade steel. Its surface is covered in materials such as Kevlar, the tough stuff used to make bullet-proof vests, to stop the ISS being punctured by debris flying around in orbit (see page 13).

THINKING OUTSIDE THE BOX!

Engineers are using the ISS to test ideas for safe structures for astronauts to live and work in for future space trips to more distant destinations. The Bigelow Expandable Activity Module (BEAM) is an inflatable module that has been tested there. These modules are light and small but after docking with the ISS, they expand to about 4 m long and 3.2 m in diameter.

LIVING IN THE STATION

THE INTERNATIONAL SPACE STATION HAS TO PROVIDE EVERYTHING ASTRONAUTS NEED TO SURVIVE IN SPACE FOR TYPICAL MISSIONS OF 4-6 MONTHS. AS WELL AS ELECTRICITY, CLEAN WATER, FOOD AND AIR TO BREATHE, THEY NEED PROTECTION FROM THE TEMPERATURE EXTREMES IN SPACE: 200°C IN THE DAY TO -200°C AT NIGHT!

Temperatures are kept at a comfortable 21°C on the ISS, and it is filled with air, so astronauts don't need to wear spacesuits inside. Astronauts float around inside the spacecraft instead of walking and have to strap themselves to their beds and toilets to prevent them floating around and crashing into things. They feel weightless because of microgravity (see Science Talk). Astronauts train in microgravity conditions for months before going to the ISS.

In microgravity conditions, it is easy for astronauts to move heavy objects because the objects are weightless too. Astronauts can shift big boxes and heavy equipment with just a touch of their fingers.

SCIENCE TALK

Gravity pulls all objects in the same way, however big or small they are. The reason a stone drops faster than a feather when you drop them is that air resistance makes the feather fall more slowly. In space there is no air, so the astronauts and the space station are falling at the same speed. This makes astronauts float and feel a less than normal pull of gravity, also known as microgravity.

On Earth, muscles and bones work against the force of gravity to support and move our bodies. This helps to keep them strong. To avoid losing bone mass and muscle strength because of microgravity during stays in space, astronauts exercise for two or more hours every day using a variety of gym equipment. Special straps and elastic cords hold them onto treadmills and bikes and create a downward force for them to push against, so the astronauts don't float away as they exercise.

ENGINEERING TALK

It's expensive to transport water from Earth to the ISS so recycling is vital. All waste water is collected, including the astronauts' urine, sweat and moisture from their breath. The waste water is filtered to remove impurities and contaminants to produce clean water that astronauts use to rehydrate dried food, wash or drink.

PROJECT

Design a gym for microgravity conditions in space.

- What sort of machines would you include?
- Why do you need to include machines that encourage weight-bearing exercises such as jogging and climbing?
- How would you make weight-lifting possible in microgravity conditions?

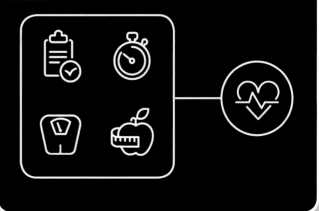

SPACEWALKS

ASTRONAUTS GO ON SPACEWALKS OUTSIDE THE INTERNATIONAL SPACE STATION TO COMPLETE TASKS SUCH AS SETTING UP SCIENCE EXPERIMENTS OR MAINTAINING THE SPACECRAFT. THEY ARE TETHERED TO THE CRAFT BY STRONG SAFETY CORDS TO STOP THEM FLOATING AWAY AND WEAR SPACESUITS FOR PROTECTION.

Spacesuits keep astronauts at a safe, stable temperature using layers of insulation and built-in pipes carrying warm or cool fluids to raise or lower temperatures when needed. The suit contains about 14 layers of different materials. One layer is made of Kevlar to protect the astronaut from space dust and debris hitting them. Another layer is waterproof and yet another is fireproof. A backpack supplies the astronaut with oxygen to breathe and removes the carbon dioxide that they breathe out.

TECHNOLOGY TALK

There are at least seven layers of Mylar® insulation in most spacesuits. Mylar® is a material often used in food storage. It helps to maintain an even temperature for astronauts by preventing heat moving in or out of a spacesuit in the same way that a Thermos™ flask or a cool box keeps food and drinks hot or cold.

Astronauts can go on spacewalks lasting several hours. They pull themselves around using handrails fixed to the exterior of the ISS and clip tools and equipment to their spacesuits or the spacecraft so they don't float away.

A device called a Simplified Aid for Extravehicular Activity Rescue, or SAFER, is attached to the back of the astronaut's spacesuit. This is like a jetpack, with several small thruster jets that can be pointed in different directions. The force of gases from a thruster in one direction moves the astronaut in the opposite one. Thrusters help astronauts get back to the ISS if they become separated from the space station.

SCIENCE TALK

On Earth, the weight of air pressing down on us is balanced by air pressure in cavities such as our lungs. As there is no air in space, there is no air pressure and this could cause the gas inside the lungs to expand and burst them. So, one layer of a spacesuit contains air that constantly presses against the astronaut's body to maintain a level of air pressure it can cope with.

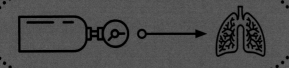

THINKING OUTSIDE THE BOX!

Many of the innovations designed for space have had a big impact on Earth too. The coatings scientists developed for space helmet visors to protect astronauts' eyes from intense sunlight are used to make the lenses in glasses, sunglasses and ski goggles ten times more scratch-resistant. Cameras developed to spot infrared light in space are now used to detect forest

WORKING IN SPACE

MANY JOBS OUTSIDE THE SPACE STATION AND OTHER SPACECRAFT ARE DONE BY ROBOTS RATHER THAN ASTRONAUTS. SPACEWALKS ARE DANGEROUS AND CAN BE EXHAUSTING FOR ASTRONAUTS. ROBOTS DO NOT GET TIRED, CAN DO TOUGHER WORK IN SPACE CONDITIONS AND ARE REASONABLY EXPENDABLE, UNLIKE PEOPLE.

The heavy duty robot on the ISS is called Canadarm2. This is a 17-m-long robotic arm. It can lift around 116 tonnes, yet is made from tough plastic just 35 cm in diameter. Canadarm2 can move around like a looping caterpillar. It can plug either of its ends into sockets all over the ISS. The sockets supply power and link to joysticks which astronauts use to control the arm's movements.

Canadarm2 is often used to grab visiting spacecraft as they fly nearby and help them dock accurately and safely with the ISS. Astronauts can view and control the exact position of Canadarm2 using colour video cameras at its joints and ends.

ENGINEERING TALK

Robotic arms are made of several long stiff pieces, rather like our arm bones, with joints linking them together that allow the arm to move. In car factories, robotic arms may have just a few parts and simple joints because they are designed to carry out simple movements. Canadarm2 has seven joints, like a human arm, but unlike human elbows and wrist joints, each can rotate fully, allowing a much wider range of movement.

Canadarm2's strength is used to help unload modules from spacecraft docked to the ISS or to hold spacewalking astronauts as they carry out more complicated jobs on distant parts of the station. Two other robots are oddjobbers. Dextre performs routine tasks on the outside of the ISS, such as changing batteries or connecting cables. Its arms are tipped with multitools such as a wrench, drill, light and camera. Robonaut works inside the ISS, wiping down handrails to avoid dirt getting into the air, checking air flow from vents and other tasks.

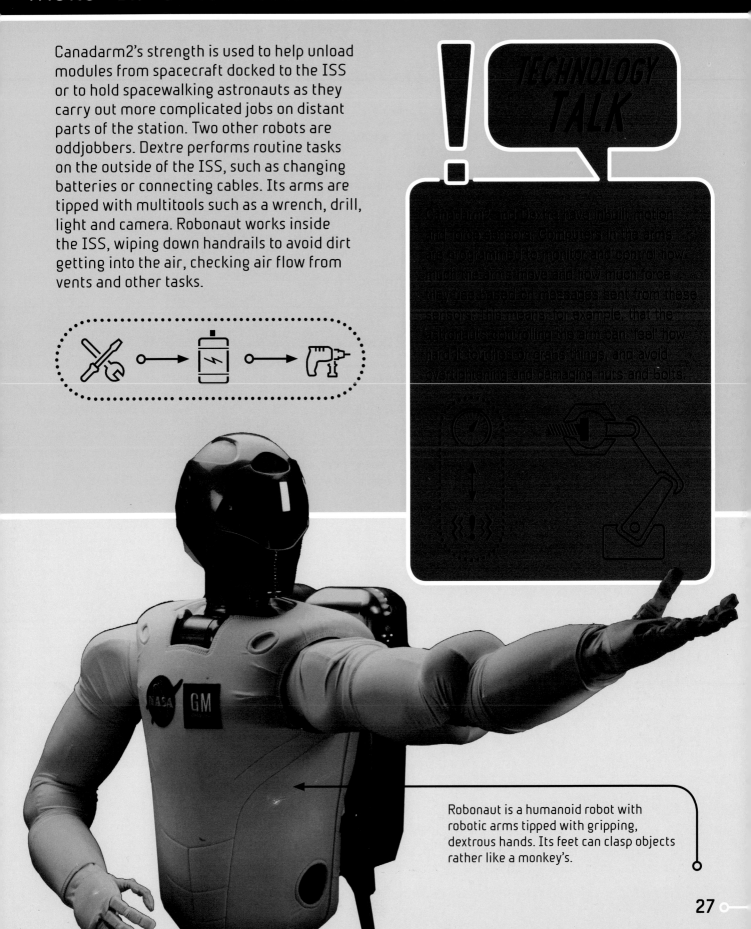

TECHNOLOGY TALK

Canadarm2 and Dextre have inbuilt motion and force sensors. Computers in the arms are programmed to monitor and control how much the arms move and how much force they use based on messages sent from these sensors. This means, for example, that the astronauts controlling the arm can feel how hard it touches or grabs things, and avoid overtightening and damaging nuts and bolts.

Robonaut is a humanoid robot with robotic arms tipped with gripping, dextrous hands. Its feet can clasp objects rather like a monkey's.

SPACE SHUTTLES

COLUMBIA, THE FIRST SPACE SHUTTLE, WAS LAUNCHED IN 1981. IT WAS USED TO TRANSPORT ASTRONAUTS AND SUPPLIES BETWEEN EARTH AND THE ISS UNTIL 2011, WHEN NASA ENDED THE SPACE SHUTTLE PROGRAMME TO FOCUS ON OTHER PROJECTS.

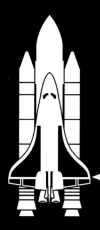

The main part of a shuttle was the orbiter, which looked like a plane, where astronauts lived and worked. The orbiter was launched from Earth with a blast from its main engine, plus pushes from two solid rocket boosters. These boosters then dropped into the ocean and could be reused. A large, orange external fuel tank attached to the orbiter fuelled its trip into orbit. Once empty, the tank dropped off and burned up on entering Earth's atmosphere.

TECHNOLOGY TALK

When returning spacecraft get closer to Earth, gravity's pull makes them speed up. Hitting the atmosphere creates friction between speeding metal and air. This friction produces air resistance that helps to slow the craft, but also enough heat to raise temperatures high enough to melt and burn metal. Discarded rocket stages are left to burn up. Space shuttle orbiters were covered with thousands of tiles made from materials that were not only insulating but also reflected heat. They could withstand temperatures of up to 1260°C.

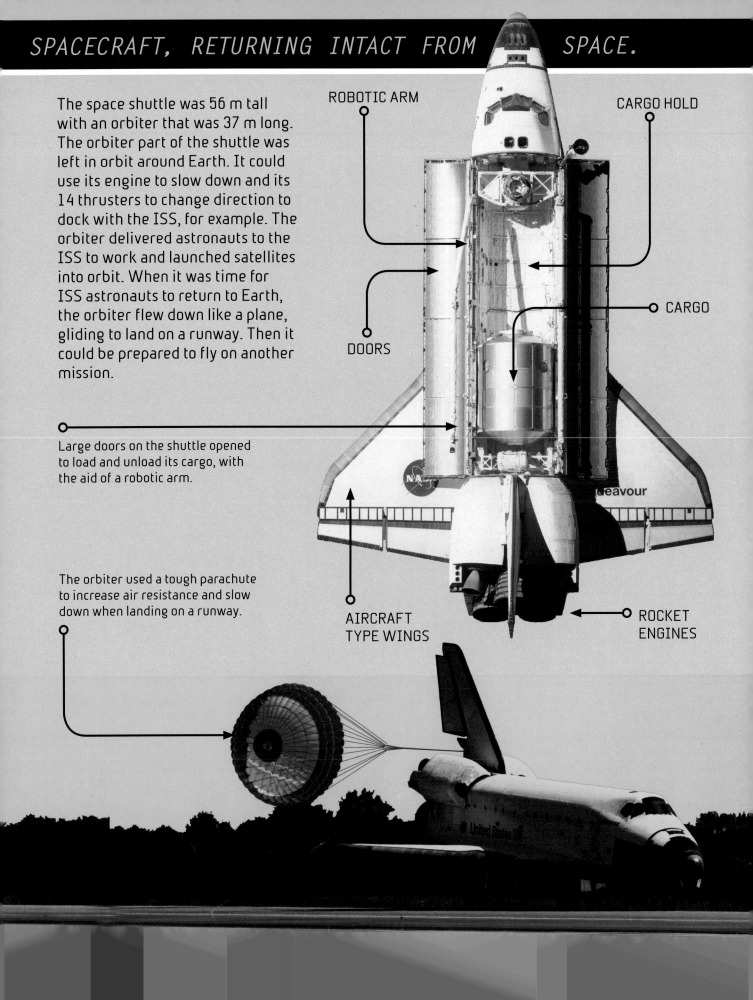

The space shuttle was 56 m tall with an orbiter that was 37 m long. The orbiter part of the shuttle was left in orbit around Earth. It could use its engine to slow down and its 14 thrusters to change direction to dock with the ISS, for example. The orbiter delivered astronauts to the ISS to work and launched satellites into orbit. When it was time for ISS astronauts to return to Earth, the orbiter flew down like a plane, gliding to land on a runway. Then it could be prepared to fly on another mission.

ROBOTIC ARM

CARGO HOLD

CARGO

DOORS

Large doors on the shuttle opened to load and unload its cargo, with the aid of a robotic arm.

The orbiter used a tough parachute to increase air resistance and slow down when landing on a runway.

AIRCRAFT TYPE WINGS

ROCKET ENGINES

HALL OF FAME: SPACECRAFT

SINCE THE DAWN OF SPACE EXPLORATION, SCIENTISTS, TECHNOLOGISTS AND ENGINEERS HAVE COME UP WITH A VARIETY OF AMAZING SPACECRAFT THAT HAVE HELPED HUMANS TO EXPLORE SPACE.

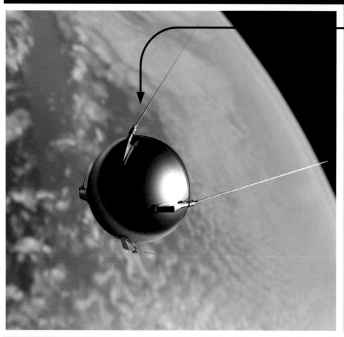

SPUTNIK 1

Sputnik 1 was the first spacecraft to orbit the Earth on 4 October 1957. It was a simple artificial satellite about the same size as a basketball. It was launched by the Soviet Union, and its name is Russian for 'travelling companion'. Sputnik 1 circled Earth every 96 minutes until early 1958, when it fell back and burned up in the Earth's atmosphere.

APOLLO 11

Apollo 11 was the first spacecraft to land men on the Moon. It launched from Florida, USA on 16 July 1969 using a Saturn V rocket. Apollo 11 had a command module, where astronauts stayed for the flight, and a lunar module, which they used to explore the Moon's surface.

MIR SPACE STATION

The Russian space station Mir was the first space station. It was assembled in orbit from 1986 to 1996, around 15 years before the ISS (see page 20). Travelling at an average speed of 28,783 kph, Mir orbited about 400 km above Earth for 15 years. Astronauts aboard Mir grew the first crop of wheat from seed in space!

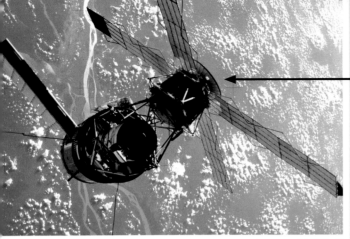

SKYLAB

Skylab was the first US space station, launched into Earth's orbit on 14 May 1973. Skylab was 30.2 m long and 6.7 m in diameter. After being visited by three crews, it started to degrade in the Sun's rays. In July 1979, it entered Earth's atmosphere and broke up, pieces of it falling into the Indian Ocean and across Australia.

SPACE SHUTTLE *CHALLENGER*

NASA had five space shuttle orbiters: *Atlantis, Challenger, Columbia, Discovery* and *Endeavour. Challenger* first launched in 1983 and made over ten missions, including that which took the first female US astronaut, Sally Ride, into space. It is sadly most famous for its final mission in January 1986, when a booster seal failed and hot gas burned through the external tank, causing a fatal explosion that killed the seven astronauts on board.

SPACEX DRAGON V2

The 7.2-m-tall SpaceX Dragon V2 is designed to carry astronauts to Earth's orbit and beyond. The first Dragon has been carrying cargo to and from the ISS since 2012, but Dragon V2 has a capsule that can carry both cargo and seven passengers into space. It can land almost anywhere on Earth, refuel and fly off again rapidly.

SPACE TELESCOPES [+]

ASTRONOMERS USE POWERFUL OPTICAL TELESCOPES ON EARTH TO VIEW STARS AND PLANETS, BUT CAN GET A FAR CLEARER VIEW BY USING SPACE TELESCOPES THAT BEAM BACK THEIR REMARKABLE VIEW.

The night sky is rarely dark on Earth because of light pollution from street lights, homes and cars. This makes dimly-lit distant objects in space harder to spot. Our atmosphere is also made from moving air that bends or refracts the light from space so objects are less clear. This is the reason why stars appear to twinkle. These effects are reduced by building observatories on high ground in places with less light pollution, or by making telescopes that use special mirrors to reduce the refraction of light from space.

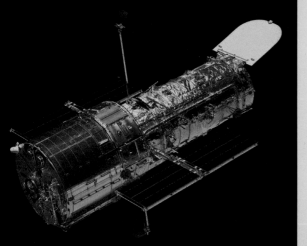

Hubble has been observing the far reaches of space from 569 km above Earth since 1990.

In space, however, telescopes can get a clearer shot of everything because there is no light pollution. Space telescopes, such as the Hubble Telescope, detect not only visible light, but also invisible light including ultraviolet and infrared. Other space telescopes can even detect the faint X-rays produced by galaxies billions of light years away. Images are sent back to Earth from space telescopes as data signals that are reconstructed into images by powerful computers.

! SCIENCE TALK

Warm objects such as the Sun give off infrared light, or heat. The clearest way to view stars and planets far away is by using the infrared they emit, rather than visible light. Scientists have devised sensors on space telescopes that can detect even tiny amounts of infrared radiation. Such technology is useless on Earth's telescopes because the atmosphere absorbs most of this radiation.

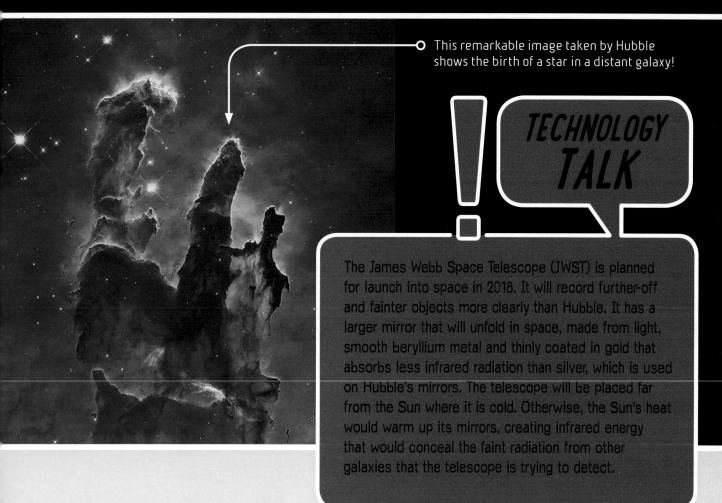

This remarkable image taken by Hubble shows the birth of a star in a distant galaxy!

TECHNOLOGY TALK

The James Webb Space Telescope (JWST) is planned for launch into space in 2018. It will record further-off and fainter objects more clearly than Hubble. It has a larger mirror that will unfold in space, made from light, smooth beryllium metal and thinly coated in gold that absorbs less infrared radiation than silver, which is used on Hubble's mirrors. The telescope will be placed far from the Sun where it is cold. Otherwise, the Sun's heat would warm up its mirrors, creating infrared energy that would conceal the faint radiation from other galaxies that the telescope is trying to detect.

MATHS TALK

Hexagons are shapes that fit together without gaps. They occur naturally in wax honeycombs made by bees to raise their young, but are also used in the JWST's mirror segments. Individual motors tilt each mirror by amounts as small as thousandths of a human hair's thickness to focus light exactly onto the JWST's sensors.

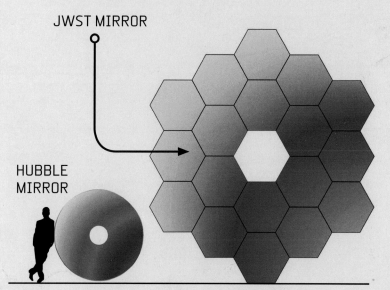

JWST MIRROR

HUBBLE MIRROR

HALL OF FAME: SPACE PHENOMENA

OVER TIME, PEOPLE STUDYING SPACE HAVE DISCOVERED MORE AND MORE ABOUT THE AMAZING SPACE PHENOMENA FOUND IN THE UNIVERSE.

BLACK HOLE

A black hole is an area in space where gravity is so strong that even light cannot escape. Gravity is so powerful in a black hole because a lot of matter is compressed into a small space, for example, such as when a star dies and collapses in on itself. Black holes themselves are invisible, but scientists can see their effects.

DWARF PLANET

A dwarf planet is a huge, spherical, natural object that orbits the Sun just like other planets. But it is much smaller. Dwarf planets are generally less than a third of the diameter of Earth. Pluto is a dwarf planet that was considered a full planet until 2006. Then, experts reclassified it as a dwarf planet because they found its gravity was too weak to pull smaller nearby objects towards it, which is a requirement for a planet.

ASTEROID

Asteroids are rocks up to 600 km wide that orbit the Sun, but are too small to be called planets. These were left over from the Big Bang 4.5 billion years ago (see page 4–5). About once a year, an asteroid as big as a car enters Earth's atmosphere, ignites into a fireball and burns up before reaching Earth's surface.

METEROID

Meteoroids are fragments of space rock that orbit the Sun. Most meteoroids burn up in a flash of light, sometimes forming a meteor shower, when they enter Earth's atmosphere. People often call them 'shooting stars'. Any meteoroids that hit Earth are called meteorites. Once every 2,000 years or so, a meteorite as big as a football field touches down somewhere on Earth! This can create massive craters and throw up giant dust clouds.

COMET

A comet is a gigantic ball of ice, dust and rock that orbits the Sun. If it strays too close to the Sun, the ice inside it condenses into gas. This forms the glowing tail we see in the night sky when a comet passes over. Many comets take hundreds or thousands of years to orbit the Sun, and very rarely pass near Earth. The famous Halley's comet is a more regular visitor, appearing every 74–79 years!

SUPERNOVA

A supernova is the explosion of a star. It is the largest explosion that happens in space. A supernova creates so much light that it can burn brighter than a whole galaxy of stars and it releases more energy than our Sun will in its entire lifetime. Supernovas are important because they release matter such as carbon and iron throughout space. Almost everything on Earth is made up of these materials.

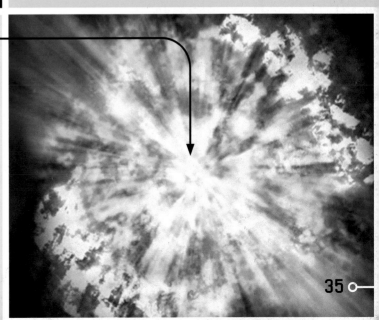

PROBES AND ORBITERS

PROBES ARE ROBOT VEHICLES THAT TAKE ONE-WAY TRIPS TO COLLECT SCIENTIFIC INFORMATION FROM THE UNIVERSE. ORBITERS ARE LIKE PROBES BUT ARE DESIGNED TO ORBIT PLANETS OR MOONS TO STUDY THEM IN GREATER DETAIL.

Probes are carried into space as rocket payload. They separate from the rocket and automatically follow courses programmed into their onboard computers, although they can often be controlled using signals from operators on Earth, too. When they reach their destination, they relay information by radio signals to Earth. This includes pictures taken by onboard cameras and data such as size of planetary features, temperatures and wind speeds in space.

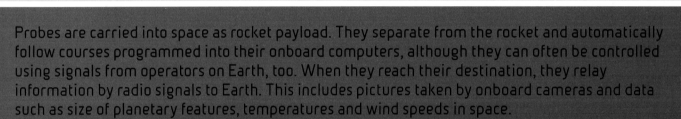

This is an artist's impression of the Voyager 1 probe. The two Voyager probes have travelled continuously since launch in 1977 at speeds of 57,000 kph, sending data about space back to Earth.

SCIENCE TALK

The Voyager probes are the most distant spacecraft from Earth. They are over 110 AU away and are reaching interstellar space, the gap between the solar system and other galaxies. Scientists keep in touch with these and other distant spacecraft using the Deep Space Network. This is a set of giant antenna dishes that can detect weak radio signals. The radio signals from the Voyager probes are 20 billion times weaker than the battery of a digital watch.

Cameras on the Cassini orbiter took this incredibly detailed image of Saturn's rings in 2013.

Orbiters circle near planets multiple times to take sequences of close-up images that show changes such as volcanic eruptions and shifting cloud patterns. Their sensors collect detailed data, such as the chemical composition of atmospheres around other planets. Probes and orbiters have discovered some amazing things. For example, Jupiter has over 60 moons, some with active volcanoes on their surface, and Saturn has wind speeds of over 1,700 kph.

THINKING OUTSIDE THE BOX!

Probes and orbiters travelling to destinations near the Sun use solar panels to produce power to move and run their instruments. But vehicles visiting the outer gas planets are moving away from the Sun, where the Sun's strength is weaker. Therefore, engineers install engines on these vehicles that convert the heat from nuclear power packs into electricity. Then they can carry on working in the darkness of space.

MATHS TALK

Mathematicians help probes and orbiters reduce travel time by calculating ways for them to hop between planetary orbits. Planets have different sizes and speeds of orbit around the Sun. It makes sense to time the trip for when they have moved closest together. A spacecraft to Mars, for example, can loop several times around Earth, accelerating faster and faster using gravity. Then, at a precisely calculated time, it exits this orbit at speed to meet up with Mars' orbit. This process is called gravity assist.

LANDERS AND ROVERS

PROBES AND ORBITERS GO CLOSE TO OBJECTS IN SPACE, BUT LANDERS ACTUALLY TOUCH DOWN ON THEM. SOME CARRY VEHICLES CALLED ROVERS DESIGNED TO EXPLORE THE OBJECT AFTER ARRIVAL. BOTH ROBOTIC MACHINES HELP PEOPLE ON EARTH TO KNOW MORE ABOUT SURFACE CONDITIONS ELSEWHERE IN THE SOLAR SYSTEM.

Landers need to be tough to survive the descent. They may have to pass through poisonous or searingly hot atmospheres around planets such as Mars and then reduce speed from very fast to a standstill without crashing. Landers gain as much information as possible about the area they land in. For example, they use robotic arms to scoop up soil, which they test for the chemicals it contains. Cameras take detailed images of the surface to help them map features such as hills, craters and valleys.

SkyCrane was a lander that lowered the rover Curiosity to the surface of Mars. It hit Mars' atmosphere at 21,000 kph and used air resistance, a parachute and downward-pointing thrusters to slow down to just 2.4 kph. Then it lowered Curiosity safely to the surface on ropes, before flying away and self-destructing.

PROJECT

Design a lander to carry a delicate object, such as an egg, from up in the air down to the ground without damage.

■ What system(s) would you use to slow the descent?

■ Which material could cushion the landing?

■ How could you protect the object inside from high or low temperatures?

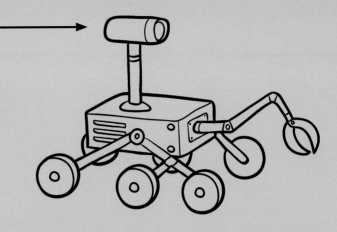

Rovers get images and data from a much wider area than landers, as they can move around. They often transmit data to their lander which may be orbiting the planet and which can communicate with Earth. These tough motorised vehicles vary in size from a microwave oven to a car. Some are steered using signals from Earth but others navigate themselves.

The first rover was driven by astronauts on Moon missions. Today's rovers are robots that move automatically across other planets and even comets.

TECHNOLOGY TALK

Operators on Earth send map references of rover destinations but a rover's onboard computer calculates the best route by comparing images taken by its cameras with stored maps and necessary data. If it meets unexpected obstacles, operators calculate and transmit the best route, but the rover also learns how to deal with similar problems for the future. Engineers use similar technology to develop smarter driverless vehicles on Earth.

MATHS TALK

In 2014, the Philae lander touched down on a speeding comet. The spacecraft carrying it (Rosetta) had left Earth in 2004. Mathematicians had to calculate where the comet was going to be ten years ahead of time, and spot a landing opportunity. Philae took seven hours to land after release from Rosetta and its speed was very carefully controlled. If its speed had been out by just 1 cm each second, then it would have been over 252 m off target, and could have fallen off the comet!

CURIOSITY

CURIOSITY IS THE MOST ADVANCED ROVER EVER BUILT. SINCE LANDING ON MARS IN 2012 (SEE PAGE 38), THE DATA IT HAS COLLECTED HAS HELPED SCIENTISTS GET ALMOST FIRST-HAND KNOWLEDGE OF THE PLANET.

Curiosity is the size of a small car. On top, there is a mast with cameras so scientists on Earth can see where it is going and what it is doing. It has a laser to blast rocks and sensors to detect what chemicals they contain. If they are of interest to scientists, operators command Curiosity to stretch out its robotic arm to collect a sample to analyse in more detail.

Curiosity's 2015 selfie shows the rocky terrain of the large Mars crater where it landed. It is still exploring that crater to this day.

ENGINEERING TALK

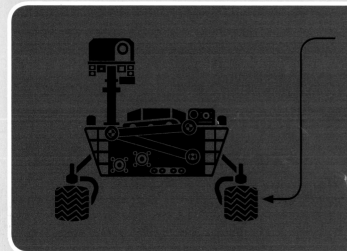

Curiosity is engineered to cope with the dusty soil and bumpy terrain of Mars. It has six large wheels with thick treads or grooves to increase friction. Each wheel has its own motor to move the rover in all directions. It also has a suspension system so springy that Curiosity can drive over obstacles 1 m high (twice as high as its wheels) while keeping all six wheels on the ground for stability.

A dried up ancient lake on Mars.

SCIENCE TALK

One of Curiosity's tasks is to look for signs of life on Mars. Until 2014, there was no evidence. But then Curiosity sampled whiffs of methane in the atmosphere. This gas contains carbon, which is a substance most living things contain. Curiosity also unearthed carbon-rich chemicals in sandy rocks on the planet. The carbon could have come from space dust, but on Earth, this gas is usually made by living things called bacteria. Could this be proof of life at last on the red planet?

ART TALK

David Hockney and other artists have produced photomontages or images made from lots of overlapping photos. Each is taken from a slightly different viewpoint and combine to create a different image than one produced from a single viewpoint. Mars teams have constructed wide-angle 'selfie' views of Curiosity and its terrain in a similar way by piecing together dozens of different photos taken by a camera on its arm.

Tools in Curiosity's arm tip include a grinder to drill holes in rocks, a spectrometer to test quantities of chemicals in rocks and a microscope for close viewing. Other sensors onboard are like artificial noses to check the gases in the atmosphere. Curiosity moves very slowly and methodically in its work. In its five years on the planet, it has covered just 15 km!

PROJECT

Produce a self-portrait using a montage of overlapping photos of your face.

■ Try using some close-ups and some wide-angle shots from varying viewpoints.

■ Think of how you could show the passage of time or family resemblances in a photomontage.

SPACE COLONIES

THERE ARE MANY REASONS WHY PEOPLE HAVE EXPLORED SPACE SO FAR, PRIMARILY KNOWING MORE ABOUT THE UNIVERSE AND LOOKING FOR SIGNS OF OTHER LIFE. THIS QUEST WOULD HAVE BEEN IMPOSSIBLE WITHOUT CUTTING EDGE SCIENCE, TECHNOLOGY, ENGINEERING, ART AND MATHS SKILLS TO SOLVE PROBLEMS. NOW PEOPLE ARE USING THEIR KNOWLEDGE OF SPACE TO PLAN FOR THE NEXT STEP: HUMAN COLONIES ON OTHER PLANETS.

Our planet is perfect at supporting life as we know it. It has an oxygen-rich atmosphere, a range of temperatures that living things can cope with, supplies of water and other natural resources. However, demand from an increasing human population is putting pressure on these resources and causing other problems, such as pollution.

Probes, orbiters and rovers have proven that Mars is the nearest planet most resembling Earth. It is rocky, has ice and other signs of water and its rocks contain mineral resources, such as iron, which is useful for building. However, the atmosphere is mostly choking carbon dioxide, it is colder than Antarctica and it has planet-wide dust storms. Technological solutions will be needed to melt Mars' ice for drinking water, produce oxygen from its atmosphere and warm colony buildings enough to grow plants for food. But life on Mars may one day be possible.

! TECHNOLOGY TALK

Mars is over 56 million km away but the furthest people have travelled from our planet is around 400,000 km. With current rockets, a human mission to Mars would take about nine months each way. The enormous weight of the launch vehicle, lander, fuel, crew, water and other life support for a complete mission is at least seven times greater than even the newest heavy-lifter launch vehicles could carry. So the only solution is to construct and take supplies to the Mars mission craft while it is in orbit.

The Space Launch System includes a rocket and the Orion spacecraft. This new system can lift 130 tonnes of cargo. It is planned for use from 2021. Orion will be eventually used for a test trip to Mars and back to Earth, kickstarting a new era of Mars exploration.

THINKING OUTSIDE THE BOX!

Towering termite mounds are constructed by millions of insects coordinating their efforts to make single complex structures. Scientists are being inspired by this cooperation in developing mini robots capable of digging and constructing in teams on Mars and other planets. For example, if one robot places its brick in one location, the next uses visual clues and its programming to put its brick next to it, on top of it or elsewhere that helps build the final construction.

SPACE TOURISM

SPACE TRAVEL IS USUALLY RESERVED FOR HIGHLY TRAINED ASTRONAUTS, BUT A NEW WAVE OF NEAR-SPACE SPACESHIPS COULD BE TAKING TOURISTS TO SPACE IN THE VERY NEAR FUTURE.

In the next few years, space tourism companies hope to start taking paying passengers beyond Earth's atmosphere. Fully trained astronauts would fly the spacecraft, taking tourists on a trip lasting about 90 minutes, up to 160 km above the Earth. Here, the tourists will experience several minutes of weightlessness and a clear view of the stars above and planet Earth below.

TECHNOLOGY TALK

Space tourism is currently only really an option for the super-rich, but new technology will allow anyone to view the wonders of space from their armchair. A satellite with wide field-of-view cameras and sensors will beam high-definition live images of space and Earth to virtual reality headsets.

One company working with the Russian national space agency has already taken passengers for ten-day trips to the ISS, at a cost of over US $20 million each. Now private companies are testing new tourist spaceship designs. Virgin Galactic's SpaceShipTwo is a reusable, winged spacecraft that is designed to repeatedly carry up to eight people, including two pilots, into space. Anyone who takes such a flight automatically receives official astronaut status.

SpaceShipTwo doesn't launch from the ground like most rockets. It is carried up to over 15,000 m by a jet aircraft. It then ignites its rocket engine and takes off on its own.

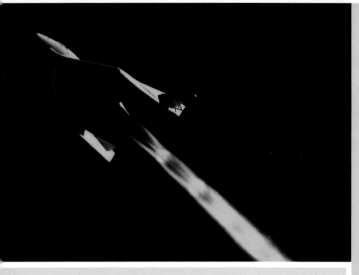

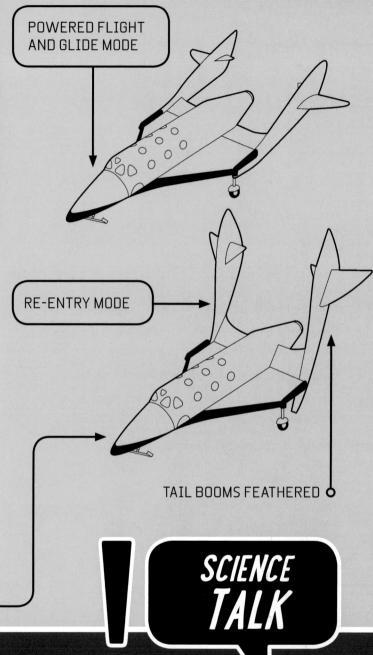

POWERED FLIGHT AND GLIDE MODE

RE-ENTRY MODE

TAIL BOOMS FEATHERED

THINKING OUTSIDE THE BOX!

SpaceShipTwo can work like a space capsule or a winged vehicle at different times during its flight. To safely re-enter Earth's atmosphere, it can reposition its wings. The tail booms move from a horizontal position to a 65-degree upright angle. This is known as feathering and it helps to slow down the spacecraft during its descent. The tail booms return to their normal position so SpaceShipTwo can glide down to land on a runway.

SCIENCE TALK

A lot of fuel is burned at rocket launches, emitting carbon dioxide. The gas and soot emitted by the rockets store the Sun's heat and warm the atmosphere. This global warming is raising average temperatures on Earth, contributing to changing weather patterns and melting polar ice. Increased global warming and climate change could be a consequence of increased space tourism in future.

GLOSSARY

aerodynamic describes something that has a shape that reduces air resistance

air pressure the push of air on the surface of objects

air resistance the force of air that slows down moving objects

asteroids large chunks of rock in the solar system

atmosphere blanket of gases around a planet

bacteria microscopic living things

black hole a place in space with such a powerful gravitational pull that even light cannot get out

carbon dioxide a gas in the atmosphere that is linked to global warming

comets objects in space made of ice, water dust and gases

drag another name for air resistance

escape velocity the speed that an object needs to be travelling to break free of a planet or moon's gravity

force a push or pull upon an object resulting from the object's interaction with another object

friction the pushing force that slows objects down when they slide against each other

galaxies huge systems of stars, dust and gases held together by gravity

GPS (Global Positioning System) a system that uses signals from satellites in space to locate positions on Earth

gravity a force pulling objects with mass together

helium a gas that is lighter than air

insulation a material that stops heat or cold passing through it

laser a narrow, concentrated and very powerful beam of light

mass the measure of how much matter is in an object

microgravity very weak gravity that creates a feeling of weightlessness

observatory a room or building that houses a space telescope

orbit the path one object in space takes around another

orbiter unmanned spacecraft that flies in orbit around a planet collecting images and data

oxygen gas in air that living things need to breathe in order to live

payload cargo carried to space on a rocket

probes unmanned spacecraft used to explore and record space

propulsion the force that moves something forwards

radiation energy in the form of waves or particles

refract to bend light

satellite electronic devices or bodies, such as the Moon, high in space that move around Earth

sensors devices that detect and measure something, such as amounts of a particular gas in the air

Soviet Union a former union of countries in Eastern Europe that included Russia

space station a large spacecraft that remains in orbit

streamlined shaped to reduce air resistance and move through the air easily and quickly

thrust a force usually produced by an engine to push a vehicle forwards

thruster an engine that creates thrust by expelling a jet of fluid or gas

X-rays a type of radiation that can pass through most materials

 # FURTHER READING

How Things Work in Outer Space Paul Mason (Wayland, 2018)

Our Universe Kevin Wood (Wayland, 2018)

Journey into Space Michael Bright (Wayland, 2018)

 # WEBSITES

FIND OUT MORE ABOUT SPACE AND SPACECRAFT, AND HOW TO GET INVOLVED AT THE FOLLOWING WEBSITES:

Learn about the universe at **www.esa.int/esaKIDSen/SEMVY5WJD1E_ OurUniverse_0.html**

Games about our solar system **www.solarsystem.nasa.gov/kids/index.cfm**

See the position of all the satellites at **www.stuffin.space**

? QUIZ

- Who invented the first rocket?

- Why can some spacecraft not run on solar power?

- What is gravity assist?

- Who was the first human in space and who was the first to walk on the Moon?

- Why do space telescopes get clearer images of the universe than telescopes

INDEX

QUIZ ANSWERS

- Robert Goddard
- They are too far from the Sun to get enough light
- Moving around one planet using its gravity to orbit and build speed to jump to another orbit
- Yuri Gagarin and Neil Armstrong
- There is less light pollution, atmospheric interference and absorption of infrared radiation

BUILDINGS

- Starting out ■ Materials
- Structure ■ Arches and domes
- Designing a building ■ Scale and plans ■ Perspective ■ Ancient buildings ■ Greeks and Romans
- Castles and cathedrals ■ Architects
- Houses ■ Eco-friendly buildings
- Skyscrapers ■ Landmarks
- Public buildings ■ Bridges
- Famous bridges ■ Tunnels
- When things go wrong
- Hostile conditions

COMPUTERS

- A Computer is... ■ Computers everywhere ■ Ones and zeros
- A computer's brain ■ Memory
- Inputs ■ Outputs ■ Programming
- Early days ■ Computer scientists
- Software ■ Graphics ■ Games
- Personal computers ■ Networks
- The web ■ Virtual reality
- Artificial intelligence ■ Amazing computers ■ A changed planet
- Future computers

MATERIALS

- Choosing Materials ■ Natural or Manmade ■ Solid ■ Liquid ■ Gas
- Rocks and Minerals ■ Wood
- Metal ■ Glass ■ Building
- Plastics ■ Ceramics ■ Textiles
- Art ■ Composites ■ Chemicals
- Super Materials ■ Special Surfaces
- Shape Changers ■ Recycling
- Future Materials

ROBOTS

- Designing a robot ■ Moving parts
- Circuits ■ Sensors ■ Sight and navigation ■ Code ■ Programming robots ■ Artificial intelligence
- Robot ethics ■ The first robots
- Robots in danger ■ Robots in space
- Drones and cars ■ Real robots
- Household robots ■ Robots and medicine ■ Bionics ■ Robotic arms
- Androids ■ Fictional robots

SPACE

- Learning about space ■ Our solar system ■ Stars ■ Galaxies and the universe ■ Comets and meteors
- Black holes ■ The Big Bang
- Astronomers ■ Observatories and telescopes ■ Space exploration
- The science of space ■ Astronauts
- Training for space
- The International Space Station
- Space walks ■ Rockets ■ Rovers
- Space probes ■ Satellites
- Space colonies ■ Future exploration

VEHICLES

- Designing a vehicle ■ Land vehicles ■ Bicycles ■ Cars
- Famous cars ■ Trains ■ Watercraft
- Boats and ships ■ Hovercraft
- Aircraft ■ Aeroplanes
- Helicopters ■ Extreme terrain vehicles ■ Power ■ Materials
- Speed ■ Braking ■ Safety features
- Style ■ Record breakers
- Vehicles of the future